A Practical Guide to Food Law in the United Kingdom

Third Edition

Ian Thomas is a dual-qualified food lawyer practising in England and Wales (barrister at Gough Square Chambers London, called to the Bar in 1993) and in the Republic of Ireland (solicitor at Ian Thomas Associates, admitted to the Roll in 2006).

Ian has substantial experience in advising clients and representing them in court across a broad spectrum of food law issues. These include: safety and hygiene, food information, slaughterhouses, animal welfare, nutrition and health claims, food supplements, borderline products, traceability, withdrawals and recalls, official controls, detention of food and challenges to enforcement actions.

He works with other lawyers and clients from outside the UK and Ireland to advise them on both domestic and EU law and policy.

Ian is a Visiting Professor at Ulster University where he contributes to lectures and course material on the PgC/PgD/MSc Food Regulatory Affairs and Veterinary Public Health courses.

He is an elected Fellow of the Society of Food Hygiene and Technology, a member of the Food Law Group, the Institution of Occupational Safety and Health and the Health and Safety Lawyers' Association.

Ian co-wrote a chapter in Consumer and Trading Standards Law and Practice ('the Pink Book') and he is a regular contributor to the European Food and Feed Law Review (Ireland country correspondent).

He is the author of two food law books published by Law Brief Publishing: 'A Practical Guide to the Law Relating to Food – Third Edition'; and 'Covid-19 and the Law Relating to Food in the UK and Republic of Ireland: The Essential Guide'.

Ian is recognised as a leading junior in both Chambers and Partners and the Legal 500.

"My go-to food law barrister. Ian can easily distil complicated and technical food points into digestible information. He has an excellent and refreshing advocacy style that he is always adapting." – Chambers UK Bar 2024

"Ian Thomas is extremely responsive and can distil technical points into easily digestible bites. He's also excellent for the instructing solicitor as he manages expectations really well." – Chambers UK Bar 2024

"An excellent advocate, who is able to advise the client on the best legal route, whilst recognising the commercial realities of the client's business." – Chambers UK Bar, 2023

"He is very client-friendly and unbelievably responsive, with excellent attention to detail." – Legal 500, 2023

A Practical Guide to Food Law in the United Kingdom

Third Edition

Ian Thomas

Barrister-at-Law, Gough Square Chambers, London

Solicitor, Ian Thomas Associates, Republic of Ireland

Law Brief Publishing

Published 2024 by Law Brief Publishing, an imprint of Law Brief Publishing Ltd
30 The Parks
Minehead
Somerset
TA24 8BT

www.lawbriefpublishing.com

Paperback: 978-1-916698-61-1

A special thanks to everyone who has supported, guided and encouraged me throughout my career. There are far too many to mention but, hopefully, you know who you are.

Sincere thanks must also go to Garry and Tim at Law Brief Publishing.

PREFACE

It is nearly four years since the UK ceased to be a member of the European Union (IP Completion Day was 31 December 2020).

Since 1 January 2021 Great Britain has been subject to a different food regulatory regime, albeit one that still is largely based on the substance of the laws and rules that applied when the UK was a member of the Union.

As is well-known, Northern Ireland is part of the United Kingdom but for most practical food law purposes, it continues to be governed by current EU food law requirements.

Previous editions of this book provide detailed information about UK food law in the immediate aftermath of Brexit. It is therefore unnecessary to go into detail about the intricacies of 'EU Exit' Regulations.

However, for readers who do not know the detail of post-Brexit UK food law, it is perhaps sufficient to say the following.

Following the referendum held on 23 June 2016, United Kingdom voters decided to leave the European Union and 'go it alone'. The margin was very tight with 52% of voters in favour and 48% against leaving.

Without in any way making a political statement, there have been many consequences of that decision which were possibly not explained clearly enough during the campaign and some which have come as a surprise to some.

It was not possible to create a whole raft of new food laws to replace the existing EU ones and so the decision was taken to keep a significant proportion of EU legislation (e.g. EU Regulations) but amend them to remove references to EU institutions (e.g. the Commission and the European Food Safety Authority) and replace them with UK-specific terms (e.g. the 'appropriate authority').

In broad terms, food law in Great Britan that is based on previous EU Regulations applies the version of those Regulations that was in force and applicable in the UK on IP Completion Day. This was known as retained law but from 1 January 2024 is now referred to as assimilated law (section 5 of the Retained EU Law (Revocation and Reform) Act 2023.

Pre-existing EU food law that was contained in Directives was not retained and reference must be made to the UK legislation that gave effect to that Directive.

By way of example, Regulation 178/2002, the general food law regulation was retained and remained part of UK law after IP Completion Day. The applicable version in Great Britain is the one in force at that date. Domestic law amended that version of the EU Regulation as necessary to remove references to matters that were no longer applicable (e.g. the Rapid Alert System) or to institutions that ceased to be relevant (e.g. EFSA) or to terms that were outdated (e.g. references to 'the Community').

Domestic application and enforcement of the EU Regulation is contained in the Food Safety and Hygiene (England) Regulations 2013 (similar Regulations apply in Scotland and Wales).

Food supplements law at EU level was, and remains, contained in Directive 2002/46/EC. European Union Directives were not carried over, or retained, as part of UK law post-Brexit. Therefore, the substantive law that applies in Great Britain is contained in the Food Supplements (England) Regulations 2003 (similar Regulations apply in Scotland and Wales).

Northern Ireland food law remains based on the current EU versions of the applicable legislation. Domestic food laws in Northern Ireland include the Food Safety (Northern Ireland) Order 1991 and the Food Hygiene Regulations (Northern Ireland) 2006.

Some of the practical consequences of no longer being a member of the EU are most keenly felt in trade between the UK and the EU. It is no longer seamless and frictionless, and it has led to increased costs and delays in the movement of foods between the two jurisdictions.

From an import and export perspective, the United Kingdom is now treated as a Third Country and is subject to the restrictions that apply to goods entering the EU from countries across the world.

This book does not cover trade, import or export in detail but readers will find the implications for border checks and controls contained in the Border Target Operating Model.

There have been signs of divergence between the laws and policies of the UK and the EU and this is likely to increase over time.

However, despite the upheaval that followed the UK's departure from the EU, it is important to appreciate that the basic rules demanding a high level of protection of human life and health and the protection of consumers' interests remain at the forefront of food law and policy in the UK as they do in the EU.

Although those aims and objectives remain the same, how they are fulfilled and the mechanisms by which they are fulfilled have changed.

This book focusses on the domestic food law system that applies in the UK. Nevertheless, it is important to acknowledge that this is firmly based on the solid foundations created by EU food law and policy. Developments at EU level and at UK level will have an impact on the future for food law in both jurisdictions and hence for us as consumers.

The law in this book is based on legislation in force on 30 September 2024.

Ian Thomas
October 2024

CONTENTS

CHAPTER ONE

AN INTRODUCTION TO FOOD LAW TERMS

Introduction

The term 'food law' covers a wide range of topics. It includes legal concepts of safety, hygiene and labelling, and broader policy issues including health, food security and sustainability.

This chapter focusses on some of the main terms and concepts that practitioners often come across when advising clients. This is based primarily on my own experience and therefore I offer my pre-emptive apologies if I have missed something that could have been included.

Part of the reason for writing this chapter in this way is to recognise that legislation often 'imports' definitions from elsewhere.

For example, section 1 (1) of the Food Safety Act 1990 states; 'In this Act "food" has the same meaning as it has in Regulation (EC) No. 178/2002'.

On other occasions, the legislation might use a term that it does not define, but referring to another piece of legislation might help in understanding the concept. For example, as will be seen shortly, the definition of 'food' includes 'processed, partly processed or unprocessed'. Those words are not defined in Regulation 178/2002 but guidance may be found in the definitions set out in Regulation 852/2004 on the hygiene of foodstuffs.

Although the UK is no longer a member state of the European Union, some of the key definitions are taken from EU legislation, now referred to as assimilated law, that applied when the UK finally ended its relationship with the EU (31 December 2020). References in this chapter to EU legislation are to that version.

Assimilated law contains amendments to the EU legislation that were needed to remove unnecessary references to EU institutions (e.g. the European Food Safety Authority – EFSA) and to make them UK-specific (e.g. by referring to the new roles of the Food Standards Agency and Food Standards Scotland, for example in relation to regulated products and health claims).

Northen Ireland food law continues to be regulated by the current versions of EU food law and hence by current EU food policy.

Assimilated law

The following references are to EU Regulation 178/2002, the General Food Law Regulation.

The purpose of food law (article 1 and article 5)

Food law has two main consumer-focussed objectives:

- A high level of protection of human life and health; and
- The protection of consumers' interests, including fair practices in food trade, taking account of, where appropriate, the protection of animal health and welfare, plant health and the environment.

Food must be safe (hence the saying, 'if it isn't safe, it isn't food').

Food must be as described.

Food law must also have regard to the effective functioning of the UK market.

Food (article 2)

> "food' (or 'foodstuff') means any substance or product, whether processed, partially processed or unprocessed, intended to be, or reasonably expected to be ingested by humans'.

Having regard to the objectives, it is not surprising to find a broad definition of food.

Food includes drink, chewing gum and any substance, including water, intentionally incorporated into the food during its manufacture, preparation or treatment. It includes water after the point of compliance as defined in Article 6 of Directive 98/83/EC and without prejudice to the requirements of Directives 80/778/EEC and 98/83/EC.

Food does not include:

(a) feed;

(b) live animals unless they are prepared for placing on the market for human consumption;

(c) plants prior to harvesting;

(d) medicinal products within the meaning of Council Directives 65/65/EEC and 92/73/EEC (now Directive 2001/83/EC);

(e) cosmetics within the meaning of Council Directive 76/768 (now Regulation (EC) 1223/2009);

(f) tobacco and tobacco products within the meaning of Council Directive 89/622/EEC (now Directive 2014/40/EU);

(g) narcotic or psychotropic substances within the meaning of the United Nations Single Convention on Narcotic Drugs, 1961, and the United Nations Convention on Psychotropic Substances, 1971;

(h) residues and contaminants.

Points (d) and (e) can arise in relation to so-called 'borderline' products. These are products where the intention is to market them as a food but due to their function or description, they cross the border and come within the legal definition of a medicinal product or a cosmetic product.

For example, a food must not be labelled as preventing, treating or curing a human disease (article 7 of the Provision of Food Information to Consumers Regulation 1169/2011). If it was so described, it might come within the definition of a medicinal product by presentation (regulation 2 of the Human Medicines Regulations 2012).

Article 3 of Regulation 178/2002 contains many important definitions;

Food law (article 3 (1))

> 'means the laws, regulations and administrative provisions governing food in general, and food safety in particular, ...; it covers any stage of production, processing and distribution of food, and also of feed produced for, or fed to, food-producing animals'.

Food business (article 3 (2))

> 'means any undertaking, whether for profit or not and whether public or private, carrying out any of the activities related to any stage of production, processing and distribution of food'.

Food business operator (article 3 (3))

> 'means the natural or legal persons responsible for ensuring that the requirements of food law are met within the food business under their control'.

This is an essential term applicable in many areas of food law. This person has the primary obligation to ensure that food law is complied with in their businesses (e.g. article 17 of Regulation 178/2002 and article 3 of Regulation 852/2004).

The food business operator will be the subject of investigations, enforcement action and, ultimately, criminal prosecution in the event of any non-compliances.

The food business operator may be a company or an individual. An individual who is a food business operator may be investigated and prosecuted. With a corporate food business operator, that may be investigated and prosecuted in that capacity, directors and other senior people may be investigated and prosecuted as individuals by being company officials.

There may be more than one food business operator. This can be seen from the above definition and was clarified in the case of *The Queen on the application of Rasool v Tower Bridge Magistrates' Court* [2013] EWHC 4736 (Admin).

Placing on the market (article 3 (8)

> 'means the holding of food or feed for the purpose of sale, including offering for sale or any other form of transfer, whether free of charge or not, and the sale, distribution, and other forms of transfer themselves'.

Risk (article 3 (9))

> 'means a function of the probability of an adverse health effect and the severity of that effect, consequential to a hazard'.

Articles 3 (10) – (13) cover risk analysis, risk assessment and risk management

Hazard (article 3 (14))

> 'means a biological, chemical or physical agent in, or condition of, food or feed with the potential to cause an adverse health effect'.

Hazard and risk are fundamental concepts in many areas of food law. They inform the preparation of the food safety management system (HACCP), they can determine whether enforcement action is taken and, ultimately whether consumers may be affected by the actions of the food business operator. Risk of harm (along with actual harm) plays an important role in the sentencing exercise.

Failure to properly identify a hazard may result in there only being a nebulous concept of a 'risk of a risk'. This may not be sufficient.

Much has been said and written about hazard and risk. For present purposes it may be sufficient to say three things.

There must be a hazard before there can be a risk. Expert involvement may be required to comment on whether a hazard exists. If so, is there a risk and if so, what is the extent of the risk for consumers' health?

Second, reference may be made to an often-cited example, one version of which may be found on the website of the BfR, the German Federal Institute for Risk Assessment.

A tiger is a hazard. If the tiger is locked securely in a cage, it creates no risk to humans. If the tiger is behind a fence, which it is capable of jumping, there is a risk to humans who are on the other side of the fence (assessing the level of risk includes many factors including whether the tiger has recently been fed!). If the tiger is free and a human being is in close proximity, the risk of harm increases (by how much also depends on an assessment of several factors – is the tiger hungry, is the human provoking the tiger etc.).

Finally, the evidence required to show a hazard and risk may depend on the situation. A low standard of proof may be sufficient to justify the taking of action to protect public health (e.g. a Hygiene Emergency Prohibition Notice) whereas the same evidence may not be sufficient to support a criminal prosecution (requiring proof beyond reasonable doubt).

Final consumer (article 3 (18))

> 'means the ultimate consumer of a foodstuff who will not use the food as part of any food business operation or activity'.

Food law often refers to the 'average consumer' who is someone reasonably well-informed, reasonably observant and circumspect.

General food law – domestic legislation

The Food Safety Act 1990 remains the overarching domestic food legislation. It is supported by a series of topic-specific statutory instruments which also apply investigation and enforcement provision of the Act and of assimilated law.

Section 1 (1) states that "food" has the same meaning as it has in Regulation 178/2002.

Section 1 (3) defines "business" which:

> 'includes the undertaking of a canteen, club, school, hospital or institution, whether carried on for profit or not, and any undertaking or activity carried on by a public or local authority.'

A "commercial operation" in relation to any food or contact material (separately defined in section 1) means any of the following –

(a) selling, possessing for sale and offering, exposing or advertising for sale;

(b) consigning, delivering or serving by way of sale;

(c) preparing for sale or presenting, labelling or wrapping for the purpose of sale;

(d) storing or transporting for the purpose of sale;

(e) importing and exporting

Section 1 (3) of the FSA 1990 continues:

"food business" means any business in the course of which commercial operations with respect to food or food sources are carried out;

"food premises" means any premises used for the purposes of a food business.

Premises is then defined to include:

> 'any place, any vehicle, stall or moveable structure and, for such purposes as may be specified in an order made by the Secretary of State, any ship or aircraft of a description so specified.'

Certain provisions in the FSA 1990 refer to sale or selling (e.g. section 14). For the purposes of the Act, "sale" is defined in section 2 (1) to include:

(a) the supply of food, otherwise than on sale, in the course of a business; and

(b) any other thing which is done with respect to food and is specified in an order made by the Secretary of State

shall be deemed to be a sale of the food, and references to purchasers and purchasing shall be construed accordingly.'

The concept of 'placing on the market, as defined in Regulation 178/2002, is broader than this.

Section 3 (2) of the FSA 1990 contains an important presumption that:

> "Any food commonly used for human consumption shall, if sold or offered, exposed or kept for sale, be presumed, until the contrary is proved, to have been sold or, as the case may be, to have been or to be intended for sale for human consumption."

Section 3 (3) continues the presumptions:

(a) any food commonly used for human consumption which is found on premises used for the preparation, storage, or sale of that food; and

(b) any article or substance commonly used in the manufacture of food for human consumption which is found on premises used for the preparation, storage or sale of that food,

shall be presumed, until the contrary is proved, to be intended for sale, or for manufacturing food for sale, for human consumption.

In a food incident where food is suspected of being non-compliant or unsafe, it is crucial to quarantine it away from other food and mark it clearly as not for human consumption (or similar wording). This rebuts the presumption and might avoid any issues about the status of that food.

Conclusion

Reference to the legal definitions is necessary when advising clients and when responding to any regulatory actions by the competent authorities.

For example, it may be that the authority is investigating or might even have prosecuted X as being the food business operator. This may be based on the officers having engaged with someone (individual or corporate representative) during an inspection or over time. X might challenge this by saying that, having regard to the legal definition they are not the food business operator for that premises or for that activity.

If a dispute cannot be resolved between the parties, a judge may be required to intervene. They will then have regard to the letter of the law and how it is to be applied in the circumstances.

CHAPTER TWO

FOOD LAW IN THE UK

Introduction

Having defined some of the broad food law concepts, it is now necessary to explain briefly how food law is regulated, administered and enforced in the United Kingdom.

As has been seen in the previous chapter, EU food law remains a major influence over food law in the UK. However, as the UK is now more able to set its own agenda, there exists the potential for UK food law and policy to move away from that in the EU. This is known as regulatory divergence and it may enable the UK to move forward with ideas that have not found favour in the EU.

Conversely, the EU might decide to make legal changes which do not accord with UK (GB) policy.

However, UK businesses who trade with the EU have found that leaving the EU has created challenges that did not exist during membership of the EU. Regulatory divergence may be positive for the UK, but it must take account of the realities of trade and the increased financial and administrative burdens on business.

Where regulatory divergence exists, food business operators might have to apply the more stringent requirements to enable their products to be sold in the UK and in the EU.

The United Kingdom

Four nations make up the United Kingdom; England, Wales, Scotland and Northern Ireland.

While they work as a unified body for the benefit of consumers, the nations have devolved administrations having responsibility for different areas of food law and policy.

To facilitate trade within the United Kingdom, the United Kingdom Internal Market Act 2020 applies a form of domestic mutual recognition in which goods may trade freely between the nations.

This is like the EU principle that goods lawfully made and marketed in one member state may be sold in another member state.

Both of those general rules are subject to certain limited restrictions.

In a food law context, the United Kingdom is divided between Great Britain (England, Wales and Scotland) and Northen Ireland.

<u>Great Britain</u>

As alluded to elsewhere in this book, EU food legislation that was retained after the UK left the EU remains in force in Great Britain but only in respect of the version that applied at IP Completion Day (31 December 2020). For our purposes this applies mainly to EU Regulations.

That EU 'retained' legislation is now referred to as 'assimilated law' (section 5 of the Retained EU Law (Revocation and Reform) Act 2023). Assimilated law includes the versions of EU Regulations 178/2002 (general food law), 852/2004 (hygiene of foodstuffs) and 1169/2011 (food information to consumers) in force in the UK on 31 December 2020

When in force, section 6 of the 2023 Act introduces new rules setting out when the courts can depart from assimilated case law (the intention is to make it easier for the UK courts to move away from decisions of the Court of Justice of the European Union).

Northern Ireland

For reasons that are well-known and need not be repeated, Northern Ireland was treated separately for food law purposes (and indeed for other laws).

Northern Ireland follows current EU food law and policy. Full details can be found in the Withdrawal Agreement and in the Protocol on Ireland/Northen Ireland (see Annex 2 for the full list of contemporary EU food legislation that applies in Northern Ireland). The operation of the Protocol is now subject to developments in the Windsor Framework.

This has resulted in some differences in approach between Northern Ireland, being governed by EU food law and Great Britain.

Titanium dioxide is an additive used in foods (E171). In 2022, the EU institutions determined that it was no longer safe to be used and it was banned (this included in Northern Ireland). However, the authorities in Great Britain took a different view and its use was not banned there.

Food as a devolved policy area

The UK four-country working model is subject to the devolved policy responsibilities of the individual nations.

The devolved policy areas are:

1) Food and feed safety and hygiene;

   England – Food Standards Agency (FSA)

Wales – FSA

Northern Ireland – FSA

2) Nutrition and health claims and nutrition labelling

England – Department of Health

Wales – Welsh Government

Northern Ireland – FSA

3) Food compositional standards and labelling

England – Department of Environment, Food and Rural Affairs

Wales – FSA

Northern Ireland – FSA

In Scotland, Food Standards Scotland has responsibility and works closely with the FSA to achieve consumer safety and consumer protection (see the FSA/FSS Memorandum of Understanding).

Reference might also be made to the FSA's publication 'Potential Divergence of Food Safety Regulations Within the UK' which sets out their approach to four-nation working within the context of devolution.

Making EU food law applicable in Great Britain

The previous edition of this book provides some detail about how retained, now assimilated, EU food law was amended to make it relevant to and applicable in Great Britain.

An example may be useful to show how this was achieved.

As the EU institutions ceased to have jurisdiction in Great Britain and to reflect Great Britain's place outside the EU, article 3 (19) was inserted into Regulation 178/2002 by regulation 7 of the General Food Law (Amendment etc.) (EU Exit) Regulations 2019 (post-Brexit amendments to EU law can usually be found in regulations with 'EU Exit' in their title).

Article 3 (19), as inserted, states:

"appropriate authority" means—

a. in relation to England, the Secretary of State;
b. in relation to Wales, the Welsh Ministers;
c. in relation to Scotland, the Scottish Ministers;

Article 3 (20) was also inserted by those EU Exit Regulations:

"third country" means any country or territory other than the British Islands.

Unfortunately, 'British Islands' is not defined in the food legislation and its definition is to be found in Schedule 1 to the Interpretation Act 1978 when the phrase is defined as:

'the United Kingdom, the Channel Islands and the Isle of Man.'

Versions of assimilated law can be found on the Legislation UK website and include references to the 'EU Exit' regulations that made the amendments or insertions.

Notification, registration and approval of food businesses

Notification and registration

Article 6 (1) of assimilated Regulation 852/2004 requires food business operators to cooperate with the competent authorities in accordance with the law appliable in each constituent territory of Great Britain.

To that end, article 6 (2) of Regulation 852/2004 states that food business operators must notify, at least 28 days before trading or operations start, the appropriate competent authority (usually a local authority) of each establishment under their control that carries out any of the stages of production, processing and distribution of food, with a view to the registration of each such establishment. This is done by means of an online form at https://register.food.gov.uk/new.

This enables the competent authority to undertake appropriate official controls including conducting risk-based inspections.

When a food business makes any 'significant change in activities', article 6 (3) of Regulation 852/2004 requires this to be notified to the competent authority and, if the risk to consumers has increased, this may result in more frequent inspections. The competent authorities must submit a notification if any establishment closes.

The requirement to notify applies to 'any unit of a food business' (article 2 (1) of Regulation 852/2004).

Approval

The above process of notification and registration simply means that the food business operator is telling the competent authority that it is, or strictly speaking will be, operating a food establishment in the authority's area.

However, the process is different and more complex where food business operators place products of animal origin on the market. In this case, the establishment generally requires positive permission before it can operate. It must be approved by the competent authority (article 6 (3) of Regulation 852/2004 and article 4 of Regulation 853/2004).

Approval is required from the Food Standards Agency (e.g. slaughterhouses and cutting plants) or a local authority (e.g. cold stores, meat products processing plants and establishments handling fish, dairy and eggs). It is important to check which is the relevant competent authority for the specified activity.

Approval is very formal and is required before the establishment starts operating (otherwise the activity is taking place in an unapproved establishment and this can lead to significant consequences such as withdrawal or recall of food products, enforcement, prosecution and, most importantly, risks to consumer health).

The application for approval may be refused or if granted it may be conditional or full. Once granted, the approval may be suspended or withdrawn.

Reference should be made to article 148 of assimilated Regulation 2017/625 (the Official Controls Regulation) for further information regarding approval. For the making of appeals in respect of approval decisions, see regulation 12 of the Official Feed and Food Controls (England) Regulations 2009.

General

In addition to the potential issues and consequences mentioned above, non-compliance with the notification, registration and approval requirements is a criminal offence (see regulation 19 (1) and Schedule 2 of the Food Safety and Hygiene (England) Regulations 2013) (see chapter ten).

Regulation of products

Many products, referred to as 'regulated products', may only be placed on the market if they have been authorised.

Prior to Brexit, the European Food Safety Authority (EFSA) played a significant role in the assessment and authorisation regulated products.

Since Brexit, the responsibility for receiving applications for authorisation and conducting the risk analysis has fallen to the Food Standards Agency and Food Standards Scotland.

The FSA and FSS are the competent authorities in respect of applications for new regulated product authorisations (and re-authorisations where required) for the market in Great Britain. In respect of such products being placed on the market in Northern Ireland, the EU application and authorisation process continues to apply.

Regulated products include; additives, flavourings, food contact materials, genetically modified organisms, novel foods, smoke flavourings and CBD products.

A full analysis of the process and procedure for obtaining regulated product authorisation is outside the scope of this book. Readers are referred to the websites of the FSA/FSS which provide detailed and helpful guidance covering both general matters and specific product types.

Regulated products is an area partly dependent on scientific developments and policy considerations. For example, on 30 September 2024, the European Food Safety Authority published updated guidance for novel foods and safety assessments. The UK authorities will need to decide whether is reliance on a previous version of the EFSA guidance is suitable and sufficient.

Potential applicants may seek guidance by contacting the FSA at regulatedproducts@food.gov.uk.

The following is no more than a general overview. References to the FSA include references to FSS and both work with interested parties during the process.

- Application submitted and is checked to ensure all required information has been provided;
- The application is subject to a risk analysis – risk assessment (hazard and risk, risk management and risk communication);
- A safety assessment is undertaken and relevant evidence and scientific information is analysed (by FSA/FSS and their Joint Expert Groups and Scientific Advisory Groups);
- Having obtained, reviewed and analysed all relevant information, the FSA considers whether to recommend to ministers that the application is approved or refused;
- Ministers make the final decision to either refuse the application or grant it. If granted, the authorisation is then confirmed in legislation and entered in the register of authorised products;
- The Applicant is told about the decision

Although a key focus of the process is protecting human health, other relevant factors include any impact on the environment, on animal welfare and on food security.

Regulated products consultation

In April 2024, the FSA/FSS issued a joint consultation on two aspects of the regulated products process. Now the FSA/FSS are responsible for the authorisation process they felt that changes were required to ensure that applications are dealt with efficiently and to cope with innovation in the food industry.

The two consultation issues are:

1. To remove the requirement to renew authorisations in respect of feed additives, GMO foods and smoke flavourings;

2. To allow regulated product authorisations to come into effect when the decision is published rather than having to wait until legislation was made. The time between publication of the ministerial decision to grant authorisation and the enacting of legislation confirming that decision can be at least three months. Additionally, the procedure for making secondary legislation (Statutory Instruments) is different between England, Wales and Scotland which can create challenges in making the necessary legislation.

The consultation ended on 5 June 2024 and further developments are awaited.

Regulation of nutrition and health claims

A detailed discussion of nutrition and health claims is contained in chapter six.

For present purposes, it is sufficient to note that this is another area in which the approval process for Great Britain has moved from the EU institutions to the domestic 'appropriate authorities' who are required to maintain a Register of nutrition of nutrition and health claims made on food (article 20 of assimilated Regulation 1924/2006).

Article 2 (2) of that Regulation defines 'appropriate authority' as:

- In relation to England – the Secretary of State;

- In relation to Scotland – the Scottish Ministers; and
- In relation to Wales – the Welsh Ministers

Northern Ireland continues to be governed by the EU institutions and procedures.

For practical purposes, nutrition and health claims contained in the EU Register at 1 January 2021 (i.e. those which had been fully evaluated and a final determination made of any application for authorisation) are now included in the GB Register.

Therefore, if advising on a GB health claim issue, reference must be made to the GB Register. For claims in Northern Ireland and the EU, reference must be made to the EU Register.

Applications seeing authorisation of a health claim in Great Britain are made by completing an application form and sending it to the Department of Health and Social Care, (the Secretary of State being the appropriate authority). Applications for a claim to be authorised in England, Scotland or Wales only are submitted to the relevant appropriate authority (see above).

Upon receipt of an application for authorisation of a health claim, the UK Nutrition & Health Claims Committee (UKNHCC) publishes a Scientific Opinion (like the Scientific Opinions published by the European Food Safety Authority (EFSA).

Two UKNHCC Scientific Opinions were published in August 2024 and can be found at https://www.gov.uk/government/collections/uknhcc-scientific-opinions. They provide an interesting read and show the approach taken by the UKNHCC and the extent to which this is like the approach taken by EFSA.

- Proposed health claim – 'Daily creatine supplementation can contribute to improved cognitive function' – Conclusion – 'the

Committee concludes a cause -and-effect relationship has not been established between the consumption of ≤3g per day creatine and improved cognitive function.'

- Proposed health claim – Consumption of beta-glucans from oats or barley contributes to the reduction of the glucose rise after a meal – Conclusion – 'the Committee agrees that the evidence is insufficient to demonstrate a cause-and-effect relationship between beta-glucan (across different types and sources) and reduction of postprandial glycaemic response at doses ≤2g per 30g avCHO.'

The applications were unsuccessful

Applications for new nutrition claims for use in Great Britain or in England, Scotland or Wales only, are submitted to the same appropriate authority as for health claims.

Conclusion

The food regulatory landscape in the UK is not as simple and straightforward as it may at first appear. This can create confusion for food businesses looking to enter the UK market and this can be particularly important where they want to have a presence in Great Britain and in Northern Ireland.

The Food Standards Agency and Food Standards Scotland have taken on the responsibility for regulating products and claims. The application processes and procedures are, for obvious reasons, based on those in place within the EU.

However, as time progresses, the UK and the EU must ensure that the regimes in place in their jurisdictions continue to be suitable to meet their legal, regulatory and consumer protection obligations.

Decisions in respect of regulated products may be subject to legal challenge. For an example, in respect of novel foods, regard may be had to the decision in *The King on the application of Guilin GFS Monk Fruit Corporation and Food Standards Agency and Food Standards Scotland* [2024] EWHC 614 (Admin).

CHAPTER THREE

FOOD SAFETY

Introduction

As the Food and Agriculture Organisation of the United Nations observes; 'If it isn't safe, it isn't food'.

Food business operators are legally obligated to produce and supply safe food. Consumers expect that the food they eat will be safe.

In addition to the applicable version of EU legislation (assimilated law in Great Britain and current EU law in Northern Ireland), reference must be made to the domestic law (e.g. the Food Safety Act 1990 and statutory instruments applicable in the four nations of the UK).

This chapter sets out the key legal provisions relating to food safety. Other aspects of safe food production, including hygiene requirements, may be found in other chapters.

As in other chapters, references to EU legislation in Great Britain is to the assimilated law versions namely those which were in force at 31 December 2020.

The principles of food safety

<u>Regulation 178/2002</u>

Article 14 sets out the key concepts and definitions and it is therefore necessary to consider the article in full.

Non-compliance with article 14 is a major determining factor in the food business operators' obligation to notify, withdraw and/or recall food (see chapter seven) and may lead to a criminal prosecution (see chapter ten).

Food must not be unsafe

Article 14 (1):

> 'Food shall not be placed on the market if it is unsafe'.

The prohibition relates to 'placing on the market' which is defined in article 3 (8):

> "placing on the market' means the holding of food or feed for the purpose of sale, including offering for sale or any other form of transfer, whether free of charge or not, and the sale, distribution, and other forms of transfer themselves.'

This is very broadly drafted and accords with the general concept of ensuring consumer protection at all stages of the food supply chain. It is much wider than simply selling or supplying food which is unsafe.

When is food 'unsafe'?

Article 14 (2):

> 'Food shall be deemed to be unsafe if it is considered to be:
>
> a. injurious to health;
>
> b. unfit for human consumption.'

Injurious to health implies that food will or may be harmful (e.g. due to the presence of a pathogen or a physical object such as glass).

Unfit for human consumption implies that the food is unacceptable in some way; it would not be reasonable to expect the food to be consumed in that state (e.g. due to the presence of foreign objects, a taint – smell or taste or deterioration leading to decay or mould).

Food may be both injurious and unfit.

If a hazard has been identified, the next step is to assess the risk associated with that hazard. Articles 14 (3) and (4) assist this process.

Determining whether food is unsafe

Article 14 (3):

> 'In determining whether any food is unsafe, regard shall be had:
>
> a. to the normal conditions of use of the food by the consumer and at each stage of production, processing and distribution, and
>
> b. to the information provided to the consumer, including information on the label, or other information generally available to the consumer concerning the avoidance of specific adverse health effects from a particular food or category of foods.'

Conditions of use includes whether the food should be cooked before consumption. Consuming raw chicken is likely to be injurious to health. However, under normal conditions, chicken would only be consumed after it has been cooked properly. Raw chicken is therefore not injurious within the meaning in article 14 (1).

Correct cooking instructions are therefore essential. Consumers at put at risk if that label fails to tell the consumer how to properly cook the chicken or if a label fails to provides proper information about the presence of allergens.

Determining whether food is injurious to health

Article 14 (4):

In determining whether any food is injurious to health, regard shall be had:

a. not only to the probable immediate and/or short-term and/or long-term effects of that food on the health of a person consuming it, but also on subsequent generations;

b. to the probable cumulative toxic effects;

c. to the particular health sensitivities of a specific category of consumers where the food is intended for that category of consumers.

This indicates that food may be injurious if consumed now (e.g. due to a high level of a pathogen) or over time (e.g. due to the presence of a carcinogenic substance).

Sub-article (c) is relevant to consumers who may be intolerant or allergic to a substance where there has been a failure to warn consumers that a product contains the substance that might cause them harm. The rules relating to the provision of food information in respect of specified allergens is contained in chapter five.

Determining whether food is unfit for human consumption

Article 14 (5):

> 'In determining whether any food is unfit for human consumption, regard shall be had to whether the food is unacceptable for human consumption according to its intended use, for reasons of contamination, whether by extraneous matter or otherwise, or through putrefaction, deterioration or decay.'

As noted above, the assessment is now primarily one of unacceptability rather than the likelihood of causing injury to health. This may be due to the smell associated with decomposing food or something physical such as a fingernail. Food may be unacceptable and create a risk to health (for example mouldy food).

Unsafe food as part of a batch

Article 14 (6):

> 'Where any food which is unsafe is part of a batch, lot or consignment of food of the same class or description, it shall be presumed that all the food in that batch, lot or consignment is also unsafe, unless following a detailed assessment there is no evidence that the rest of the batch, lot or consignment is unsafe.'

This enables the competent authority to seize or detain a whole consignment based on the test results of a batch. The food business operator is left to try to show that parts of the consignment that were not tested are not tainted by those negative results. This might be way of testing the remaining parts of the consignment to show they are compliant or not unsafe or perhaps by showing that the negative results were caused by an ingredient which was not used to produce the whole consignment. This is not an easy task but the circumstances may highlight that this is worth exploring.

Food complying with food legislation

Article 14 (7) is the applicable article.

There are differences in the wording in the assimilated version (applicable in Great Britain) and the current EU version of Regulation 178/2002 (applicable in Northern Ireland). Both are set out as another example of how changes were made following Brexit.

Article 14 (7) – the current EU version

> 'Food that complies with specific Community provisions governing food safety shall be deemed to be safe insofar as the aspects covered by the specific Community provisions are concerned.'

Article 14 (7) – the GB assimilated version

> 'Food that complies with specific **legislation in force in the relevant constituent territory of Great Britain** governing food safety shall be deemed to be safe insofar as the aspects covered by the specific [...] provisions are concerned.'

The words in bold were substituted by the General Food Law (Amendment etc.) (EU Exit) Regulations 2019. The words in [...] were omitted by the same EU Exit Regulations.

Despite the changes, the basic operation of article 14 (7) is the same in the EU/NI and in GB.

This may be seen by adopting the contrary position to the wording of the sub-article.

If food does not comply with the applicable legislation then it is deemed to be unsafe, unless a specific risk assessment proves otherwise (see for example the criteria in articles 14 (3) – (5)).

A food may contain a substance at a higher level that permitted by legislation. That legislation would be contravened, but the risk assessment would determine whether it also in breach of article 14 (is it injurious or unfit). If yes, the obligations around notification, withdrawal and/or recall will be engaged.

If the risk assessment determines otherwise, the specific legislation may have been contravened but the food may not be unsafe.

Competent authorities may still take measures even when food conforms with legal provisions

Article 14 (8) states:

> 'Conformity of a food with specific provisions applicable to that food shall not bar the competent authorities from taking appropriate measures to impose restrictions on it being placed on the market or to require its withdrawal from the market where there are reasons to suspect that, despite such conformity, the food is unsafe.'

It should be noted that competent authorities are permitted to make consumers aware of potential risks to human or animal health (article 10 of Regulation 178/2002 – 'public information').

Where there are no specific provisions

Article 14 (9) of the current EU version of Regulation 178/2002 states:

> 'Where there are no specific Community provisions, food shall be deemed to be safe when it conforms to the specific provisions of national food law of the Member State in whose territory the food is marketed, such provisions being drawn up and applied without prejudice to the Treaty, in particular Articles 28 and 30 thereof.'

Article 14 (9) was omitted from the assimilated version of Regulation 178/2002 by the same EU Exit Regulations referred to above.

<u>Food Safety Act 1990</u>

The FSA 1990 was affected by the UK's membership of the EU, not least because of the food safety requirements set out in article 14 of Regulation 178/2002. The provisions of the FSA 1990 in respect of food safety are used less frequently than article 14 of Regulation 178/2002.

Nevertheless, the FSA 1990 remains good law.

Rendering food injurious to health

Section 7 (1) of the FSA 1990 states;

> 'Any person who renders any food injurious to health by means of any of the following operations, namely—
>
> (a) adding any article or substance to the food;
>
> (b) using any article or substance as an ingredient in the preparation of the food;
>
> (c) abstracting any constituent from the food; and
>
> (d) subjecting the food to any other process or treatment,
>
> with intent that it shall be sold for human consumption, shall be guilty of an offence.'

The continued influence and importance of EU food law and Regulation 178/2002 can be seen in section 7 (2) (as amended by the General Food Informations 2004):

> 'In determining for the purposes of this section whether any food is injurious to health, regard shall be had to the matters specified in sub–paragraphs (a) to (c) of Article 14(4) of Regulation (EC) No. 178/2002.'

Article 14 (4) is set out in full above.

Conclusion

Food may be unsafe if it is harmful or simply because it would not be reasonable to expect it to be consumed in its condition.

A food may be unsafe because it is both harmful and unacceptable.

It may be very important to be clear about why it is alleged, or accepted, that food is unsafe. This may impact the decision-making process of the food business operator, the competent authority and, if applicable, the court.

Producing safe food involves applying different elements of food law and the next chapter considers one of the most important; food hygiene.

CHAPTER FOUR

FOOD HYGIENE

Introduction

Poor hygiene practices inevitably lead to risks to food safety.

Maintaining proper levels of food hygiene at all stages of the food supply chain is an essential part of legal compliance and consumer protection.

Non-compliance with food hygiene rules should not happen but where it does it features very highly in decisions to take enforcement action (e.g. closing food businesses) and by being the foundation of criminal prosecutions (e.g. unclean premises, contamination of food and the presence of pests being high on the list).

Food business operators must make themselves familiar with the rules and engage suitable and competent staff, consultants and contractors to enable them to be fully compliant. They must create and maintain a positive food safety culture in which everyone does the right thing, all the time, where or not they are being supervised.

Assessing and evaluating potential breaches of the hygiene rules and the consequences that might follow hygiene often requires correctly identifying the hazard and then the extent of the risk of harm that flows from the hazard (see chapter one).

Other relevant laws include assimilated Regulation 2073/2005 on microbiological criteria for foods. This is a method of checking the safety of food and the suitability and acceptability of processes.

Responsibility for compliance

As noted elsewhere in this book, 'primary responsibility for food safety rests with the food business operator' (article 1 (1) (a) of Regulation 852/2004).

Article 3 of that Regulation states: 'Food business operators shall ensure that all stages of production, processing and distribution of food under their control satisfy the relevant hygiene requirements laid down in this Regulation.'

When things go wrong, the competent authorities will focus their attention on the food business operator and the systems and procedures, or lack of them, within the business.

The hygiene rules and basic principles

As stated in the third recital to Regulation 852/2004, 'experience has shown that [the general rules of hygiene for foodstuffs and the procedures for verification of compliance with these rules] constitute a sound basis for ensuring food safety.

The overarching philosophy of the food hygiene rules is to set out the requirements and objectives to be met while allowing the food business operator a degree of flexibility in how to achieve the regulatory objectives. A 'one size fits all' approach cannot work.

Measures can then be put in place to meet all legal requirements and, perhaps the food business operator may seek to implement systems that amount to best practice and go beyond simple compliance.

The main rules on the hygiene of foodstuffs are set out in article 1 (1) of Regulation 852/2004. Having stated that the food business operator bears primary responsibility, the article lists the following hygiene principles:

- ensuring food safety throughout the food chain, starting with primary production;

- maintaining the cold chain for foods that cannot be stored safely at ambient temperatures;

- implementing procedures based on the HACCP principles (Hazard Analysis and Critical Control Points – a food safety management system);

- using guides to good practice as a means of helping to secure compliance with hygiene rules and application of the HACCP principles;

- establishing microbiological criteria and temperature control requirements based on a scientific risk assessment;

- ensuring that imported foods are of at least the same hygiene standard as food produced in Great Britain, or are of an equivalent standard.

Emphasising the importance of food hygiene along the food supply chain, article 1 notes that the Regulation applies 'to all stages of production, processing and distribution of food and to exports and without prejudice to more specific requirements relating to food hygiene'.

Non-application of the general hygiene rules in Regulation 852/2004

The Regulation does not apply to:

- primary production for private domestic use;

- the domestic preparation, handling or storage of food for private domestic consumption;
- the direct supply, by the producer, of small quantities of primary products to the final consumer or to local retail establishments directly supplying the final consumer; and
- collection centres and tanneries which fall within the definition of food business only because they handle raw material for the production of gelatine or collagen.

The general scheme of Regulation 852/2004

Key definitions in Regulation 852/2004

Article 2 of the Regulation contains key definitions including:

'food hygiene', hereinafter called 'hygiene', means the measures and conditions necessary to control hazards and to ensure fitness for human consumption of a foodstuff taking into account its intended use; and

'contamination' means the presence or introduction of a hazard.

The Annexes to the Regulation prescribed various duties and obligations that food business operators must abide by.

Food business operators' obligations

Adopting the general theme of responsibility and accountability in food law, article 3 states:

> 'Food business operators shall ensure that all stages of production, processing and distribution of food under their control satisfy the relevant hygiene requirements laid down in this Regulation.'

FBOs carrying our primary production must comply with the general hygiene provisions in Annex I and any specific requirements provided for in Regulation 853/2004 in respect of foods of animal origin (article 4 (1))

FBOs carrying out a carrying out any stage of production, processing and distribution of food after those stages to which paragraph 1 applies shall comply with the general hygiene requirements laid down in Annex II and any specific requirements provided for in Regulation (EC) No 853/2004 (article 4 (2)).

In addition to those general hygiene requirements, article 4 (3) states:

'Food business operators shall, as appropriate, adopt the following specific hygiene measures:

a. compliance with microbiological criteria for foodstuffs;

b. procedures necessary to meet targets set to achieve the objectives of this Regulation;

c. compliance with temperature control requirements for foodstuffs;

d. maintenance of the cold chain;

e. sampling and analysis.'

Article 5 of Regulation 852/2004 then provides the foundation for food hygiene namely HACCP. This is a food safety management system in which the food business operator undertakes a full review of their business to identify what they do, how they do it, who is involved and what dangers (or hazards) exist if things are not done correctly and how these can be eliminated or satisfactorily controlled.

One of the first things a regulatory official will do when entering a food business is to ask to see the food safety management system and there is a legal requirement on the FBO to provide this (article 5 (4).

The primary obligation under article 5 (1) is that the FBO must 'put in place, implement and maintain a permanent procedure or procedures based on the HACCP principles.'

These principles in article 5 (2) are worth setting out in full:

a. identifying any hazards that must be prevented, eliminated or reduced to acceptable levels;

b. identifying the critical control points at the step or steps at which control is essential to prevent or eliminate a hazard or to reduce it to acceptable levels;

c. establishing critical limits at critical control points which separate acceptability from unacceptability for the prevention, elimination or reduction of identified hazards;

d. establishing and implementing effective monitoring procedures at critical control points;

e. establishing corrective actions when monitoring indicates that a critical control point is not under control;

f. establishing procedures, which shall be carried out regularly, to verify that the measures outlined in subparagraphs (a) to (e) are working effectively;

   and

g. establishing documents and records commensurate with the nature and size of the food business to demonstrate the effective application of the measures outlined in subparagraphs (a) to (f).

The Annexes

They set out a series of obligations that must be complied with depending on whether the FBO is engaged in primary production (Annex I) or in stages after primary production (Annex II).

Non-compliance can form the basis of enforcement action and prosecution.

Article 2 (3) is an important provision when interpreting the Annexes:

'In the Annexes to this Regulation the terms 'where necessary', 'where appropriate', 'adequate' and 'sufficient' shall mean respectively where necessary, where appropriate, adequate or sufficient to achieve the objectives of this Regulation.'

Annex II consists of twelve chapters each setting out a series of obligations including cleanliness of premises and equipment, transport, food waste, water supply, personal hygiene, avoiding contamination of foodstuffs, control of pests, wrapping and packaging of foodstuffs and training.

In practice, the common allegations of non-compliance include:

- Food premises are to be kept clean and maintained in good repair and condition (Chapter I, paragraph 1);

- Every person working in a food-handling area is to maintain a high degree of personal cleanliness and is to wear suitable, clean and, where necessary, protective clothing. (Chapter VIII, paragraph 1);

- At all stages of production, processing and distribution, food is to be protected against any contamination likely to render the food unfit for human consumption, injurious to health or contaminated in such a way that it would be unreasonable to expect it to be consumed in that state. (Chapter IX, paragraph 3);

- Adequate procedures are to be in place to control pests. Adequate procedures are also to be in place to prevent domestic animals from having access to places where food is prepared, handled or stored (or, where the competent authority so permits in special cases, to prevent such access from resulting in contamination) (Chapter IX, paragraph 4); and

- Food business operators are to ensure: that food handlers are supervised and instructed and/or trained in food hygiene matters commensurate with their work activity (Chapter XII, paragraph 1).

It is important to check very carefully the nature of the alleged breach because some provisions only apply in certain circumstances. For example, Chapter II only applies to rooms where foodstuffs are prepared, treated or processed.

Sometimes assessing full compliance may require an interpretation of the provision in the context of the activities being undertaken.

Annex II, Chapter I, paragraph 4 states:

> *"An adequate number of washbasins is to be available, suitably located and designated for cleaning hands. Washbasins for cleaning hands are to be provided with hot and cold running water, materials for cleaning hands and for hygienic drying. Where necessary, the facilities for washing food are to be separate from the hand-washing facility."*

Adequate is subject to the definition in article 2 (3) as set out above.

This provision was the subject of a reference for a preliminary ruling to the Court of Justice of the European Union under Article 267 of the TFEU by the Austrian Courts in a case concerning a public house which served "almost no food, except toast". The washing facility in the premises was equipped with hot running water which could be used for washing hands but was also used for washing dishes.

The Court of Justice made the following remarks:

1. A wash basin for the purposes of paragraph 4 does not mean one that must be used exclusively for washing hands;

2. The final sentence of paragraph 4 makes clear that the same basin may be used for washing hands and for washing food, otherwise there would be no need to require that, where necessary, hands and food must be washed in separate equipment;

3. As the phrase "where necessary" must be read having regard to the objectives of the rules, it is not necessary to have a washing facility exclusively for washing hands where there is a facility for washing food (it all depends on the circumstances, the hazards and the risks and what steps are needed to protect consumers).

See *Astrid Preissl KEG v Landeshauptmann von Wien* (Case C-381/10).

Another case heard by the Court of Justice is also instructive as to the approach to interpreting and applying the food hygiene legislation.

In *Albrecht and others v Landeshauptmann von Wien* (Case C- 382/10).

The applicable provision in that case was Annex II, Chapter IX, paragraph 3;

> *"At all stages of production, processing and distribution, food is to be protected against any contamination likely to render the food unfit for human consumption, injurious to health or contaminated in such a way that it would be unreasonable to expect it to be consumed in that state."*

1. The Austrian authorities directed traders to install containers for the self-service supply of bread and bakery products so they could only be removed using technical means such as tongs, and once items had been removed, they could not be replaced;

2. The risk identified by the authorities was that the containers, which were already in use in Germany without undue cause for concern, allowed customers to touch and remove the products by hand, or cough or sneeze on them and could replace product which they had already removed. These activities could cause germs to be deposited on the products;

3. The authorities did not present evidence of actual contamination of the products;

4. Experts in Germany and Austria opined that the use of the containers did not create hygiene problems and as such it was reasonable for the traders to have regard to this when selecting the containers for use;

5. In all the circumstances the Court stated that:

    - it cannot be concluded that food business operators have infringed paragraph 3 on the basis only of the finding that a potential purchaser could conceivably have touched the foodstuffs by hand or sneezed on them;

    - it was necessary to consider the food safety management system implemented by the traders under Article 5 (to prevent, eliminate or reduce to acceptable levels the hazards); and

    - the authorities must determine that the food safety management system was insufficient in the light of all the available relevant information.

The mere presence of a risk that someone might sneeze on the bread, which might cause contamination, and might replace the bread was, on the facts of the case, insufficient to show a breach of chapter IX, paragraph 3.

Hygiene of foodstuffs – laying down specific hygiene rules for food of animal origin – Regulation 853/2004

Article 1 (1) of Regulation 853/2004 states that the Regulation, "lays down specific rules on the hygiene of food of animal origin for food business operators. These rules supplement those laid down by Regulation 852/2004. They shall apply to unprocessed and processed products of animal origin."

General non-application of Regulation 853/2004

Regulation 853/2004 does not apply to:

a) primary production for private domestic use;

b) the domestic preparation, handling or storage of food for private domestic consumption;

c) the direct supply, by the producer, of small quantities of primary products to the final consumer or to local retail establishments directly supplying the final consumer;

d) the direct supply, by the producer, of small quantities of meat from poultry and lagomorphs slaughtered on the farm to the final consumer or to local retail establishments directly supplying such meat to the final consumer as fresh meat;

e) hunters who supply small quantities of wild game or wild game meat directly to the final consumer or to local retail establishments directly supplying the final consumer; and

f) retail (although there are particular rules applying to retail that must be examined on a case-by-case basis – see for example Article 1(5))

Rules governing the activities referred to in paragraphs (c), (d) and (e) are set by the appropriate authority (as defined above) (Article 1 (4)).

Guidance on the application of the various exemption criteria can be found in FSA publications such as its Operational Policy for the Approval of Establishments.

Definitions for the purposes of Regulation 853/2004

For the purposes of applying the Regulation, Annex I contains important definitions including; meat, live bivalve molluscs, fishery products, milk, eggs, frogs' legs and snails.

'Products of animal origin' means: food of animal origin, including honey and blood; live bivalve molluscs, live echinoderms, live tunicates and live marine gastropods intended for human consumption; and other animals destined to be prepared with a view to being supplied live to the final consumer.

Under the heading "meat" in Annex I, are definitions of "mechanically separated meat" (paragraph 1.14) and "meat preparations" (paragraph 1.15). These seemingly innocuous terms have been the subject of a long series of cases before the English Courts and upon a preliminary reference to the Court of Justice of the European Union and readers may find the discussion and debate of interest particularly regarding the Courts' approaches to legislative interpretation and the scope of an English court (see *R (on the application of Newby Foods Limited) v Food Standards Agency [2019] UKSC 18* and the decision of the CJEU *(C-453/13)*).

Some other aspects of Regulation 853/2004

Premises/establishments

Only products prepared and handled exclusively in establishments that meet the applicable requirements of food law and have been registered or, where required, approved by the competent authority may be placed on the market (Article 4).

With certain exceptions, establishments handling products of animal origin for which Annex III to Regulation 853 lays down specific requirements (e.g. transporting and slaughtering animals) require approval by the relevant competent authority before they can operate (see chapter two).

Annex III covers products of animal origin including: meat from various animals (cattle, pigs, poultry, lagomorphs and game); minced meat, meat preparations, meat products and mechanically separated meat; fish, milk, eggs and frogs' legs and snails. It sets out, in many respects quite detailed, requirements covering many aspects of production of these products such as the layout of premises), hygiene matters, compositional requirements and labelling.

Product marking

Product of animal origin may only be placed on the market if it has been handled in an establishment subject to approval and it has either:

(a) a health mark applied in accordance with Regulation (EC) No 854/2004;

or

(b) when that Regulation does not provide for the application of a health mark, an identification mark applied in accordance with Annex II, Section I, of this Regulation

Conclusion

Operating a compliant food business depends on having proper food safety management systems in place and following all applicable hygiene rules.

Although staff can be trained to understand the law and to undertake certain responsibilities, they need to be made to feel part of a team. They need to appreciate that what they do and don't do has an impact on their colleagues and ultimately the business as a whole.

Developing a positive food safety culture alongside solid and robust food safety management systems will go a long way to creating the foundations for a compliant and successful business.

CHAPTER FIVE

FOOD INFORMATION TO CONSUMERS

Food information, or labelling as it used to be called, empowers consumers to make informed choices about the food they choose.

It fulfils key objects of food law by:

- protecting the health of consumers who may be adversely affected by food (e.g. providing information about allergens);
- protecting consumers' interests (e.g. health by providing nutrition information or other choices such as vegetarian or vegan or environmental information);
- preventing consumers from being misled (e.g. country of origin);
- preventing consumers from being deceived (e.g. paying more for specialty foods such as honey when the product is fake or not of the appropriate standard); and
- protecting consumers from eating unsafe food (e.g. instructions for storage and cooking)

Food information may be divided between information that is mandatory and that which is provided voluntarily, and between the rules for prepacked food and non-pre-packed.

It may also be divided between information required by general rules applicable to foods (having horizontal effect) and that which is also required for specific foods such as chocolate (having vertical effect).

General food information rules are also relevant to various policy areas including health (e.g. high fat, sugar and salt) and environmental matters (e.g. eco-claims and greenwashing).

Some terms used in the provision of food information are not governed by legislative requirements but may be subject to 'generally accepted' definitions (e.g. vegetarian/vegan) or less 'generally accepted' definitions (e.g. 'natural', 'pure' or fresh'). In such circumstances, regard may be had to judicial interpretations or to rulings made by the Advertising Standards Authority and similar organisations.

Even so, there remains the potential for differences of opinion what a term is intended to mean in a particular set of circumstances.

This chapter reviews some of the main legal provisions that govern the provision of food information to consumers. References are to assimilated law, Regulation 1169/2011 on the Provision of Food Information to Consumers ('FIC').

Mandatory food information

Article 9 of FIC provides a list of mandatory particulars for pre-packed foods and article 10 prescribes 'additional mandatory particulars for specific types or categories of food'.

Article 9 (1) – the list of mandatory particulars

Subject to specified exceptions, the following particulars are mandatory.

a) the name of the food;

b) the list of ingredients;

c) any ingredient or processing aid listed in Annex II or derived from a substance or product listed in Annex II causing allergies or intolerances used in the manufacture or preparation of a food and still present in the finished product, even if in an altered form;

d) the quantity of certain ingredients or categories of ingredients;

e) the net quantity of the food;

f) the date of minimum durability or the 'use by' date;

g) any special storage conditions and/or conditions of use;

h) the name or business name and address of the food business operator referred to in Article 8(1);

i) the country of origin or place of provenance where provided for in Article 26;

j) instructions for use where it would be difficult to make appropriate use of the food in the absence of such instructions;

k) with respect to beverages containing more than 1,2 % by volume of alcohol, the actual alcoholic strength by volume;

l) a nutrition declaration.

Article 9 then prescribes how those particulars must be indicated.

Article 10 – additional mandatory particulars

These must be provided in respect of the specific types or categories of foods set out in Annex III.

Annex III products are:

- foods packaged in certain gases;
- foods containing sweeteners;
- foods containing glycyrrhizinic acid or its ammonium salt (liquorice);

- beverages with high caffeine content or foods with added caffeine;
- foods with added phytosterols, phytosterol esters, phytostanols or phytostanol esters; and
- frozen meat, frozen meat preparations and frozen unprocessed fishery products

Detailed rules for providing mandatory food information

Further information for the provision of mandatory food information is contained in articles 11 to 35 of FIC and these should be referred to when considering how to present that information.

They include general provisions including:

Article 12	mandatory food information shall be available and shall be easily accessible in accordance with [FIC], for all foods
Article 13	mandatory food information shall be marked in a conspicuous place in such a way as to be easily visible, clearly legible and, where appropriate, indelible. It shall not in any way be hidden, obscured, detracted from or interrupted by any other written or pictorial matter or any other intervening material
Article 14	provisions regarding distance selling (i.e. prepacked foods offered for sale by 'means of distance communication' – defined in article 2 (2) (u))
Article 15	language requirements – mandatory food information shall appear in English (or in English and other languages)
Article 16	omission of certain mandatory particulars

Detailed rules for the provision of the mandatory information in article 9 (1) are contained in articles 17 to 35:

Article 17	name of the food
Articles 18 to 21	ingredients (including allergens – see below)
Article 22	quantitative indication of ingredients (QUID)
Article 23	net quantity
Article 24	minimum durability and use by date
Article 25	storage conditions or conditions of use
Article 26	country of origin or place of provenance
Article 27	instructions for use
Article 28	alcoholic strength
Articles 29 to 35	nutrition declaration

Voluntary food information

Article 36 (1) states that when food information referred to in articles 9 and 10 is provided on a voluntary basis (e.g. a nutrition declaration on an alcoholic beverage), that information must comply with the relevant requirement for mandatory food information.

Food information provided on a voluntary basis must:

- not mislead the consumer (see article 7 of FIC – also see article 16 of Regulation 178/2002);
- not be ambiguous or misleading for the consumer; and

- must, where appropriate, be based on relevant scientific data

(article 36 (2))

Mandatory food information takes precedence over information provided on a voluntary basis. Article 37 makes clear that voluntary food information must not be displayed to the detriment of the space available for mandatory food information.

National measures for non-prepacked food – including foods prepacked for direct sale

Article 44 of FIC states that the allergen information required by article 9 (1) (c) is mandatory; 'Where foods are offered for sale to the final consumer or to mass caterers without prepackaging, or where foods are packed on the sales premises at the consumer's request or prepacked for direct sale'.

Article 44, as amended post-Brexit, also states that domestic regulations may provide for the provision of other information required under articles 9 and 10.

Ingredients and allergens

Two issues require consideration.

Firstly, in respect of foods that are not prepacked, the food business operator may make allergen information available 'by any means the operator chooses, including [...] orally'. (regulation 5 of the Food Information Regulations 2014 – 'FIR').

Secondly, regulation 5 A of FIR specifies that foods that are prepacked for direct sale must provide a list of ingredients (article 9 (1) (b) of FIC) and details of the allergen substances used as ingredients in the food (article 9 (1) (c) of FIR).

This second provision is sometimes referred to as 'Natasha's law' as it was introduced on 1 October 2021 following the death of Natasha Ednan-Laperouse who consumed a sandwich containing sesame seed when she was allergic to that substance.

Requirement to name foods

There is a general requirement to name foods that not prepacked (regulation 6 of FIR) and foods that are prepacked for direct sale (regulation 6 A of FIR).

Providing information – allergens used as ingredients

Telling consumers that a food contains something that might harm them or might even kill them seems so obvious.

It might be thought that the rules that will soon be described are simple and straightforward, they are not always followed properly. This may be due to lack of care or understanding on the part of the food business operator, it may be due to a failure to properly identify how and when allergens might be present in food or it might be down to a failure to train and supervise staff.

In the UK, as in the EU, there are fourteen substances listed in Annex II of FIC that cause allergies or intolerances that must be indicated to consumers. The Annex should be reviewed in detail as there are several exceptions, but broadly speaking the fourteen may be categorised as:

1. Cereals containing gluten, namely: wheat (such as spelt and khorasan wheat), rye, barley, oats or their hybridised strains, and products thereof;

2. Crustaceans and products thereof;

3. Eggs and products thereof;

4. Fish and products thereof;
5. Peanuts and products thereof;
6. Soybeans and products thereof;
7. Milk and products thereof (including lactose);
8. Nuts, namely: almonds (Amygdalus communis L.), hazelnuts (Corylus avellana),walnuts (Juglans regia), cashews (Anacardium occidentale), pecan nuts (Caryaillinoinensis (Wangenh.) K. Koch), Brazil nuts (Bertholletia excelsa), pistachio nuts (Pistacia vera), macadamia or Queensland nuts (Macadamia ternifolia), and products thereof;
9. Celery and products thereof;
10. Mustard and products thereof;
11. Sesame seeds and products thereof;
12. Sulphur dioxide and sulphites at concentrations of more than 10 mg/kg or 10 mg/litre in terms of the total SO2;
13. Lupin and products thereof;
14. Molluscs and products thereof.

The list is subject to change as happened with Regulation (EU) 2024/2512 which amended point 10, mustard, which from 1 April 2025 in the EU, but not in the UK (GB) will read:

> ‘10. Mustard and products thereof, except:
>
> behenic acid with a minimum of 85 % of purity and obtained after two distillation steps used in the manufacturing of the emulsifiers E 470a, E 471 and E 477;’

The presence, or possible presence, of allergens in food should be considered within the food business's HACCP plan or food safety management system. Allergens may be listed as a separate hazard alongside chemical, microbiological and physical hazards.

Where allergens are used as ingredients in prepacked foods requiring a list of ingredients, article 21 of FIC requires that they:

a) shall be indicated in the list of ingredients with a clear reference to the name of the substance or product as listed in Annex II; and

b) the name of the substance or product as listed in Annex II shall be emphasised through a typeset that clearly distinguishes it from the rest of the list of ingredients, for example by means of the font, style or background colour.

Two points arise:

First, the consumer need only look at the list of ingredients to see if the food contains any allergenic ingredients. The label should not refer to these ingredients anywhere other than in the list of ingredients.

Second, consumers reading a food label will see something like, 'For allergens see ingredients in **bold**', or however the food business operator has chosen to emphasise the allergen.

Where the food does not contain a list of ingredients, indicating the allergen on the label is by using the word 'contains' followed by the name of the allergen (for example a wine label stating 'Contains sulphites').

The rules for providing information about allergens used as ingredients in food that is not prepacked or prepacked for direct sale are set out above.

Providing information – allergens not used as ingredients but which may be present in the final product

Sometimes there is a risk that a food may contain one of the 14 specified allergens even though they are not used as ingredients.

This may occur where food A does not contain one or more of the 14 allergens as an ingredient but is produced in the same facility as food B which does have one or more of the allergens as an ingredient.

Systems should be in place to avoid cross-contact between the foods (whether through direct contact, airborne transmission or contact via humans, materials or equipment). Nevertheless, there may still be a risk that the allergen from food B has found its way into food A.

Where this might happen, the food business operator might engage the use of precautionary allergen labelling (PAL) which is frequently seen on a label as 'may contain' followed by the name of the allergen or allergens.

This should only occur following a robust risk assessment that concludes that despite all the measures taken to prevent any cross-contact, the risk remains.

If no information is provided to consumers, the food may be deemed to be unsafe as it might be injurious to health (see above).

If too much information is provided about the risk that allergens might be present, the information could be misleading (see above) or it might be counter-productive and bad for PR. It might also limit, unnecessarily, the consumers who may wish to buy the product.

Blanket precautionary allergen labelling should never be used as a protection against litigation; we told you it may contain X allergen so you can't take legal action against us. It should also never be used to hide or cover up poor food practices.

Conclusion

Accurate food information empowers consumers to make informed decisions about which foods they purchase. This may be necessary due to health issues (e.g. allergens) or because of personal or lifestyle choices (e.g. vegetarian or vegan).

Failing to provide the correct in formation can lead to serious illness or even death and may result in consumers being misled thus adversely affecting their interests.

As noted above, deaths caused by unsatisfactory allergen labelling can lead to changes in food information law. There is a strong call for changes to providing allergen information in respect of non-prepacked foods, such as on menus. Reference may be made to the Food Standards Agency's 'Consultation on Best Practice Guidance – Allergen Information for Non-Prepacked Foods (October 2024).

Finally, there is a lot of debate about using 'meaty names' for plant-based meat substitutes. This is a complex issue but regard may be had to the decision of the Court of Justice of the European Union in Case C-438/23 – *Protéines France and others*. We wait to see the impact of the discussion around using meaty names for plant-based foods in the UK.

CHAPTER SIX

NUTRITION AND HEALTH CLAIMS

Introduction

Food businesses seek to provide ways of promoting a food, or an ingredient in food, as providing a beneficial effect on consumers generally or a specific group of consumers.

Consumers are entitled to be provided with information that is legal, accurate, open and transparent to facilitate informed decision-making.

Nutrition and health claims must comply with general conditions of use and with specific conditions applicable to each type of claim.

This chapter considers the general legal framework and then reviews some of those general and specific conditions of use.

This area of law, particularly health claims, is commonly associated with food supplements and their labelling. Regrettably, space does not allow for any detailed discussion on the regulatory requirements for food supplements.

The law

Assimilated law

The legal requirement for providing nutrition and health claims is set out in assimilated law, Regulation 1924/2006 on nutrition and health claims made on foods ('NHCR'). As with other food laws post-Brexit, this has been amended to make it relevant and applicable to the UK (GB).

As we will see, permitted nutrition claims are contained in the Annex to the NHCR and there are conditions that apply to their use.

Health claims may only be used if they have been authorised and appear in the Annex to Regulation (EU) 432/2012 or are separately authorised in accordance with Article 14 claims.

Both types of claims must also comply with general and specific legislative requirements

Domestic law

The Nutrition and Health Claims (England) Regulations 2007, as amended, provide for the administration and enforcement of the NHCR.

These Regulations specify the competent authorities (i.e. the Food Standards Agency or the relevant port health or local authority), provide for offences and penalties and apply various provisions of the Food Safety Act 1990 (as is common with many domestic food law regulations).

The 2007 Regulations have been amended by the Nutrition and Health Claims (England) (Amendment) Regulations 2024 (S.I. 2024 No. 165) which come into force on 1 October 2024.

The Amendment Regulations provide for the enforcement of specified provisions of the NHCR. Prior to these regulations, enforcement of nutrition and health claims law was quite limited (the only formal method of enforcement was a criminal prosecution which can be time consuming, costly and may not always lead to a timely rectification of any wrong-doing).

By modifying the Food Safety Act 1990, the Amendment Regulations have introduced the power to serve an Improvement Notice as an alternative to prosecution (modification of section 10 of the Food Safety Act 1990 in the new Schedule to the 2007 Regulations). Ancillary modifications of the 1990 Act are introduced including to permit appeals against the service of Improvement Notices. Some believe that this change will see a marked increase in the regulatory supervision and enforcement of nutrition and health claims law.

The modifications of the 1990 Act have also resulted in the offence of obstruction of officers now being covered by section 33 of the Act rather than regulation 7 of the 2007 Regulations.

A draft Statutory Instrument is in the pipeline which will revoke 60 pieces of tertiary legislation relating to the authorisation of health claims by the EU. This legislation no longer has any legal purpose in the UK (GB).

Regulation 1924/2006 – general definitions

In general terms, nutrition claims may only be used if they are listed in the Annex to the NHCR and are 'in conformity with the conditions set out in this Regulation' (article 8).

Health claims may only be used if they fulfil specific criteria (set out in the NHCR) and 'are authorised in accordance with this Regulation and are included in the list of authorised claims in the Annex to Commission Regulation (EU) 432/2012 or are authorised for the purposes of Article 14' (Article 10).

Commercial communications

The NHCR only applies to nutrition and health claims made in 'commercial communications' whether in the labelling, presentation or advertising of foods to be delivered as such to the final consumer It also applies to foods intended for supply to restaurants, hospitals, schools, canteens and similar mass caterers. (article 1 (2)).

The NHCR will therefore apply where the primary purpose of the communication is to induce consumers to choose a particular product, particularly where the outcome is a benefit to the business (e.g. financial).

It does not apply to non-commercial communications such as dietary guidelines or advice issued by public health authorities.

The NHCR may not apply where the primary purpose of the communication is to change consumer behaviour (e.g. by advocating an increase or decrease in consumption of specified substances where this is not done to promote or sell a particular product).

The lines can become blurred and each claim is considered on a case-by-case basis.

Claim

This is any message or representation, which is not mandatory under any enactment, including pictorial, graphic or symbolic representation, in any form, which states, suggests or implies that a food has particular characteristics (Article 2 (2) (1)).

Nutrition claim

This means any claim which states, suggests or implies that a food has particular beneficial nutritional properties due to:

a) the energy (calorific value) it

    i. provides;

    ii. provides at a reduced or increased rate; or

    iii. does not provide; and/or

b) the nutrients or other substances it

i. contains;

ii. contains in reduced or increased proportions; or

iii. does not contain;

Nutrition claims include stating that a food is a 'source of' a specified nutrient (e.g. fibre) or contains a high amount of that nutrient such as making the claim 'high fibre'.

It also relates to claims that a food contains a 'low' or a 'very low' amount of a nutrient (e.g. sodium/salt) or contains 'no added' sodium/salt.

In each case, the Annex to the NHCR includes any conditions of use for example relating to the amount of the nutrient that must be present before the claim is permitted.

Health claim

This means any claim that states, suggests or implies that a relationship exists between a food category, a food or one of its constituents and health.

Having regard to the purpose of the legislation, this is broadly interpreted.

A quick way of checking whether the claim is an authorised health claim is by reviewing the Register required by Article 20 of the NHCR (there is an EU Register and since Brexit, a separate GB Register). The Register includes applications which have been rejected.

Reference must also be made to the legislation that authorises the use of the health claim, or indeed has refused to authorise the use of a particular claim.

The Registers are broadly similar as those claims authorised pre-Brexit have been retained in the UK (GB). In time there may become a divergence between the Registers.

The health claim, 'Calcium contributes to normal blood clotting' is authorised whereas, 'Calcium helps to keep a healthy blood pressure' is not authorised.

Quite often the authorised health claims use words such as 'contributes to', 'maintains' and 'normal'. This emphasises that the substance is present to help keep things normal or the way they should be rather than stating, suggesting or implying that the substance will help to cure or alleviate a deteriorating condition or illness (this is also precluded under general food information law).

It is not always easy to ascertain which side of the line a proposed claim falls and the answer lies on a case-by-case assessment having regard to matters such as wording and context.

Regulation 1924/2006 – general requirements

General principles for nutrition and health claims

They must not (article 3):

1) be false, ambiguous or misleading (applying the general principles of food information law);

2) give rise to doubt about the safety and/or the nutritional adequacy of other foods;

3) encourage or condone excess consumption of a food;

4) state, suggest or imply that a balanced and varied diet cannot provide appropriate quantities of nutrients in general;

5) refer to changes in bodily functions which could give rise to or exploit fear in the consumer, either textually or through pictorial, graphic or symbolic representations.

Article 4 refers to the setting of nutrient profiles which has not yet come into force. These are maximum amounts for nutrients such as fat, sugar and/or salt in foods, above which the use of nutrition or health claims would be restricted or forbidden. For example, breakfast cereals exceeding a sugar limit could no longer advertise their fibre or vitamin content. Work continues at EU level to set maximum and minimum levels but it is unclear when this will be concluded and when or if definitive amounts will be set.

Reference may be made here to the nutrient profiling model used to reduce exposure to the advertising of foods high in fat, salt and sugar.

Article 5 provides a series of general conditions that must be complied with before a nutrition or health claim may be used.

The claims are only permitted if the average consumer can be expected to understand the beneficial effects as expressed in the claim and the claims must refer to the food ready for consumption.

The general conditions include reference to the need for a significant quantity of the substance for which the claim is made, the nutrient or substance must be in a form that is available to be used by the body and require compliance with any applicable specific conditions.

Chapter III sets out specific conditions for the use of nutrition claims. Article 8 notes that the list of permitted nutrition claims is contained in the Annex along with the permitted conditions of use.

Article 9 provides that comparative claims 'between foods of the same category' may be made.

Chapter IV refers to the specific conditions applicable to health claims. Article 10 states that health claims must be authorised and included in the list of authorised claims in the Annex to Regulation 432/2012 or are authorised for the purposes of article 14 (reduction of disease risk claims and claims referring to children's development and health).

Article 10 (2) requires specified information to be included in the label or in the presentation or advertising when health claims are used:

1) a statement indicating the importance of a varied and balanced diet and a healthy lifestyle;

2) the quantity of the food and pattern of consumption required to obtain the claimed beneficial effect;

3) where appropriate, a statement addressed to persons who should avoid using the food; and

4) an appropriate warning for products that are likely to present a health risk if consumed to excess.

It is permissible to refer to 'general, non-specific benefits of the nutrient or food for overall good health or health-related well-being' but only when that general statement is 'accompanied' by a specific authorised health claim (article 10 (3)).

This avoids a situation in which a food business operator makes a broad claim 'this product is good for you buy it now' as an inducement to purchase the product but without explaining why it is good for you by reference to an authorised health claim.

An example would be 'drink our healthy and tasty fruit drink'. The reference to 'healthy' is a generic claim which would be permitted if the product made, and was permitted to make, a claim such as, 'our drinks are a good source of vitamin C which contributes to the normal function of the immune system'.

There are some restrictions on the use of health claims. In addition to not permitting health claims in respect of alcoholic beverages (article 4 (3)), article 12 states:

'The following health claims shall not be allowed:

(a) claims which suggest that health could be affected by not consuming the food;

(b) claims which make reference to the rate or amount of weight loss;

(c) claims which make reference to recommendations of individual doctors or health professionals and associations other than national associations of medical, nutrition or dietetic professionals and health-related charities.'

Articles 13 and 14 describe the types of health claims that may be made:

1) Article 13 (1) – health claims describing or referring to:

   (a) the role of a nutrient or other substance in growth, development and the functions of the body 'Calcium contributes to normal muscle function'; or

   (b) psychological and behavioural functions 'Pantothenic acid contributes to normal mental performance' or

   (c) without prejudice to any enactment implementing Directive 96/8/EC, slimming or weight-control or a reduction in the sense of hunger or an increase in the sense of satiety or to the reduction of the available energy from the diet 'Glucomannan in the context of an energy restricted diet contributes to weight loss'

   (but note the claim must not refer to the rate or amount of weight loss – see above)

2) Article 13 (5) – claims based on newly developed scientific evidence or includes a request for the protection of proprietary data

3) Article 14 (1) (a) – health claims relating to the reduction of disease risk claims

   'Plant stanol esters have been shown to lower/reduce blood cholesterol. High cholesterol is a risk factor in the development of coronary heart disease'

4) Article 14 (1) (b) – health claims referring to children's development and health

   'Calcium is needed for normal growth and development of bone in children'

Applications for authorisations

Chapter two briefly refers to the procedure for making and determining applications for proposed health claims.

Applications may be made for authorisation in Great Britain as a whole or for authorisation in one of England, Scotland or Wales only (article 15 (1)).

The applications are made to the Department for Health and Social Care, Food Standards Scotland or the Welsh Government as appropriate.

It is not possible in this book to provide comprehensive information about the detail of the application process. Reference may be made to the application form published by the UK Nutrition and Health Claims Committee (UKNHCC) which guides the reader through the information required to support the application.

The UKNHCC provides scientific opinions on the substantiation of scientific evidence relating to applications.

Those scientific opinions are not too dissimilar in approach and content to the scientific opinions provided by the European Food Safety Authority in respect of applications made by EU member states and in respect of Northern Ireland. This is to be expected as the legislative purpose is similar as are the basic criteria for determining applications.

By way of example, the UKNHCC considered an application for authorisation of the proposed claim, 'daily creatine supplementation can contribute to improved cognitive function'. Having reviewed, considered and analysed the supporting information, the UKNHCC concluded that a 'cause and effect relationship' between the proposed consumption of creatine and improved cognitive function has not been established. This wording is familiar to readers who have seen negative EFSA scientific opinions.

If the scientific opinion is positive then the application is considered by the relevant ministers. If approved the health claim, its wording and any associated conditions of use are enacted into law and are entered on the GB Register of authorised health claims.

Conclusion

Nutrition and health claims regulation forms part of the overarching purpose of food law to provide honest and open information to consumers enabling them to make informed choices about the foods they eat.

It can also be used as a way of ensuring that the law does not permit claims which encourage or condone the consumption of foods that are deemed to be 'unhealthy'.

Even if the scientific opinion states that a proposed claim is justified, for example that the cause and effect relationship has been shown, legislators retain the power to intervene to prevent the use of claims based on policy.

The case of *Dextro Energy GmbH & Co. KG v European Commission* (Case T-100/15) is an example of this in action.

The proposed claim was 'glucose is metabolised within the body's normal energy metabolism'. EFSA concluded that based on the evidence submitted in support of the proposed claim a cause and effect relationship had been established between the consumption of glucose and the contribution to energy-yielding metabolism.

Nevertheless, the EU institutions refused to authorise the use of the health claim because it conveyed a 'conflicting and confusing message to consumers' because it would encourage consumption of sugars when all the scientific advice was that sugar consumption should be reduced. The proposed claim contravened article 3 (a) of Regulation 1924/2006 in that it was ambiguous or misleading. No specific conditions of use or additional warnings would not be sufficient to 'alleviate the confusion of the consumer'. The claim was therefore not authorised.

CHAPTER SEVEN

TRACEABILITY, WITHDRAWAL AND RECALL

Introduction

Protecting consumers against harm, or risk of harm, attributable to unsafe food is one of the crucial aspects of being a food business operator (FBO).

Any FBO can become impacted by a food incident whether or not of their own making. In this chapter, I have preferred to use the term 'food incident' rather than the alternative 'food crisis'.

Traceability is often referred to as knowledge of foodstuffs 'one step back' and 'one step forward'. FBOs must know where their ingredients come from and where their products go to. This helps to ensure food safety 'from farm to fork'.

When things go wrong, even if it is due to the actions or inactions of others, FBOs must be ready, willing and able to take immediate action to investigate, identify, isolate, instigate and inform.

Depending on the nature of the incident, the FBO may have to do some or all the following: investigate the issue, identify the cause of the problem, isolate the affected product (withdrawal), instigate the food's removal from consumers (recall) and inform the authorities about what they are doing to protect consumers and inform consumers where necessary.

The primary legal obligations are found in articles 18 and 19 of Regulation (EC) 178/2002 (assimilated law).

Traceability

Article 18 of Regulation 178/2002:

1) The traceability of food, feed, food-producing animals, and any other substance intended to be, or expected to be, incorporated into a food or feed shall be established at all stages of production, processing and distribution.

2) Food and feed business operators shall be able to identify any person from whom they have been supplied with a food, a feed, a food-producing animal, or any substance intended to be, or expected to be, incorporated into a food or feed.

   To this end, such operators shall have in place systems and procedures which allow for this information to be made available to the competent authorities on demand.

3) Food and feed business operators shall have in place systems and procedures to identify the other businesses to which their products have been supplied. This information shall be made available to the competent authorities on demand.

4) Food or feed which is placed on the market or is likely to be placed on the market in Great Britain shall be adequately labelled or identified to facilitate its traceability, through relevant documentation or information in accordance with the relevant requirements of more specific provisions.

The FBO must ask themselves, what are the ingredients I am bringing into my premises, from whom have I obtained them, do they match their description, are they of the required quality, are they free from contamination and are they safe.

This information should be recorded in a manner that is useful for the FBO and can be produced to the competent authorities, if requested.

If the FBO is notified of an issue with a foodstuff or an ingredient in their food supply chain, their traceability systems must enable them to identify their supplier and communicate with them without delay.

When considering the 'one step forward' aspect of traceability, the FBO is not required to identify their customers when they are the 'final consumer'.

One aspect of traceability, and the quality and safety of products, is the supplier audit. The FBO must satisfy themselves that their suppliers are complying fully with their legal obligations and have suitable and sufficient procedures in place to maintain the integrity of the food supply chain.

This is basic and commonplace in most FBOs. However, FBOs need to exercise great care when they need to change ingredients and/or ingredient suppliers, particularly where this is caused by unforeseen problems with their planned supply chains.

If they do not take sufficient care to check the authenticity and safety of the new ingredient and the new supplier, they may be introducing a new hazard which could have a significant impact on safety, information and claims.

There are some occasions where an external situation has such a widespread impact on the supply of an ingredient or foodstuff that FBOs need to introduce substitute ingredients to continue producing foods. For example, in the initial stages of the conflict in the Ukraine, the competent authorities provided guidance to FBOs giving temporary flexibility in how they could comply with food information legislation.

Although traceability systems and documentation should be reviewed and stress-tested regularly, their suitability and effectiveness may only be truly proved, or weaknesses identified, in a real-life incident when time is of the essence. If the procedures are not up to scratch it may be too late to rectify the situation and significant harm may be done to the business and more importantly to consumers.

Before moving to look at the FBO's obligations to withdraw, recall and notify, it might be helpful to identify the type of traceability information that would be expected (and be available to provide to the competent authority on request):

- Identification of the product (including required quality and other specifications);
- Name and address of the supplier (one-step back) and the customer, not final consumer (one step forward); and
- Details of delivery (date, time, quantity, batch number/identification information)

Food crises involving food of animal origin can create particular hazards for consumers. Therefore, the traceability requirements for such foods are set out in Regulation 931/2011:

- an accurate description of the food;
- the volume or quantity of the food;
- the name and address of the food business operator from which the food has been dispatched;
- the name and address of the consignor (owner) if different from the food business operator from which the food has been dispatched;
- the name and address of the food business operator to whom the food is dispatched;

- the name and address of the consignee (owner), if different from the food business operator to whom the food is dispatched;
- a reference identifying the lot, batch or consignment, as appropriate; and
- the date of dispatch.

When requested, the above information must be provided to the competent authority 'without undue delay'.

Withdrawal, recall and informing the authorities and consumers

Article 19 of Regulation 178/2002 sets out the responsibilities of food business operators.

As FBOs have an individual and collective obligation to protect consumers, article 19 (4) states:

'Food business operators shall collaborate with the competent authorities on action taken to avoid or reduce risks posed by a food which they supply or have supplied.'

Articles 19 (1), (2) and (3) should be reviewed in full as they contain full details of the actions that must be take, when and by whom to protect consumers.

(1) If a food business operator considers or has reason to believe that a food which it has imported, produced, processed, manufactured or distributed is not in compliance with the food safety requirements, it shall immediately initiate procedures to withdraw the food in question from the market where the food has left the immediate control of that initial food business operator and inform the competent authorities thereof. Where the product may have reached the consumer, the operator shall

effectively and accurately inform the consumers of the reason for its withdrawal, and if necessary, recall from consumers products already supplied to them when other measures are not sufficient to achieve a high level of health protection.

(2) A food business operator responsible for retail or distribution activities which do not affect the packaging, labelling, safety or integrity of the food shall, within the limits of its respective activities, initiate procedures to withdraw from the market products not in compliance with the food-safety requirements and shall participate in contributing to the safety of the food by passing on relevant information necessary to trace a food, cooperating in the action taken by producers, processors, manufacturers and/or the competent authorities.

(3) A food business operator shall immediately inform the competent authorities if it considers or has reason to believe that a food which it has placed on the market may be injurious to human health. Operators shall inform the competent authorities of the action taken to prevent risks to the final consumer and shall not prevent or discourage any person from cooperating, in accordance with national law and legal practice, with the competent authorities, where this may prevent, reduce or eliminate a risk arising from a food.

The food business operator and their advisers need to have in place and regularly review the food incident plan and the food incident management team.

As food incidents are, by definition, unpredictable, without a robust plan and a competent team, the food business operator risks causing significant harm to the business (additional and unnecessary financial cost and time and adverse reputational damage) and could delay action that is necessary to protect consumers.

There is a lot of guidance for operators to help set up procedures that will be effective in their businesses.

Some relevant issues that businesses might need to consider include:

1) How will consumers or the competent authorities contact the business? Will it be by telephone, email or might the issue be raised on social media?

2) The business needs to identify how those communications will be captured and acted on without delay. How are staff trained to recognise words or phrases that might indicate a problem that needs immediate attention?

3) Once the need for action has been identified, how is the message disseminated within the business? Who needs to be told and how will this be done?

4) Once this has happened, how will the business identify the facts and how they might be relevant to them? What is the food, is there any of it under the control of the business, what are the distribution channels?

5) Is the problem due to a foreign body (e.g. glass) which might indicate an internal problem with a production line that requires immediate attention. Is the problem limited to a single batch or are many batches involved?

6) Once the facts have been established, the risk analysis procedure takes place (risk assessment, risks management and risk communication);

7) Have the criteria for action in article 19 been engaged? Is there a non-compliance with food safety requirements?

8) If so, what steps need to be taken?

9) If not, or if there is some doubt about whether article 19 is strictly engaged, should the business act anyway including notifying the competent authorities whether out of an abundance of caution, as a precautionary measure, to maintain trust and reputation with the authorities and with consumers or because they place consumer safety above everything else?

10) The business should keep detailed notes, contemporaneously where possible, of all decisions taken, when and by whom, and of any actions that follow.

11) How will notifications be made to the competent authorities, when and by whom?

12) If a full consumer recall is required, how will this be managed by the business and by its customers (e.g. supermarkets and other retailers)?

13) How will the business know that all affected product is out of the supply chain and no longer available to consumers?

14) How will the business know when the situation is fully resolved?

15) Does the business need to engage in positive PR to negate any adverse effects of the incident?

Speed is of the essence, but so is accuracy in determining the facts to inform appropriate and timely decision-making.

Once the incident is concluded the business should review its procedures to see if any improvements are necessary. If they are then this should be done immediately to improve the response to any future food incidents.

There may also be financial implications that go beyond the immediate cost to the business of initiating its food incident procedures. There may be contractual issues to deal with and insurance policies may also need to be reviewed.

Conclusion

Good traceability systems are not only important in their own right for commercial purposes, but they can play a significant role in managing a food incident, particularly one involving an ingredient that has been supplied into the food business.

Making decisions about withdrawing or recalling food are not straightforward and involve a simultaneous analysis of legal, commercial, technical and quality matters. They may involve people from outside the business such as external lawyers and consultants and may also require urgent input from an appropriate expert.

Creating and maintaining a food incident plan is often overlooked in favour of just doing the job. However, there may come a time when having one will work very favourably for the business and not having one could be disastrous.

CHAPTER EIGHT

OFFICIAL CONTROLS AND ENFORCEMENT

Introduction

This chapter considers how food law is enforced in the United Kingdom.

It considers the broad concept of 'official controls' and reviews the statutory organisational basis for enforcement.

The discussion then moves to a review of two of the main types of powers afforded to competent authorities and individuals described in the applicable legislation as authorised officers or inspectors.

The chapter concludes with an assessment of the options available to a person, usually the food business operator, who is the recipient of enforcement action.

Although a form of enforcement, criminal prosecutions are considered in chapter nine.

Official Controls – assimilated law

When considering how competent authorities oversee, or control, food law, regard must be had to Regulation 2017/625, the Official Controls Regulation or OCR.

It is a very lengthy and detailed piece of legislation and is particularly relevant in terms of the checks and controls of imported products into Great Britain (see for example Chapter V and the Border Target Operating Model).

The rules around the checks made on products coming into Great Britain are complex and the dates for implementation of these checks have changed over several years. Detailed analysis of this is outside the scope of this book, but nevertheless, it is important to be aware of the various rules.

The OCR as amended post-Brexit to apply to Great Britain, uses the term 'third country' to refer to non-GB territories. In article 3, the term 'third country' 'means any country or territory outside the British Islands'.

The OCR does not further define 'British Islands' but it means 'the United Kingdom, the Channel Islands and the Isle of Man' (Schedule 1 of the Interpretation Act 1978).

As article 1 of the OCR observes, the Regulation lays down various rules including 'for the performance of official controls and other official activities by the competent authorities of Great Britain'.

Official controls are performed for the verification of various food related rules including; food and feed safety, integrity and wholesomeness at any stage of production, processing and distribution, including rules aimed at ensuring fair practices in trade and protecting consumer interests and information'.

The OCR also provides for official controls in respect of rules relating to feed and feed safety, health and welfare requirements for animals and organic product.

The OCR (article 2) relates to two different types of competent authority actions:

1) official controls to verify compliance by operators with the Regulation and the applicable rules and to verify that animals and goods meet the requirements of the above rules, including for the issuing of official certificates; and

2) other official activities relates to matters such as the control, prevention or eradication of the spread of animal disease or pests of plants and granting authorisations or approvals and the issuing of official certificates.

In practice, the dividing line is between competent authorities undertaking inspections of food premises to check operator compliance with the various rules (official controls) and competent authorities considering and issuing approvals for business handing products of animal origin (other official activities).

Title VII of the OCR sets out the rules relating to enforcement action.

Article 137 (1) requires competent authorities to give priority to actions to be taken to eliminate or contain risks to human, animal and plant health, animal welfare or, as regards GMOs and plant protection products, also to the environment.

Where there is a suspicion of non-compliance with the applicable rules, competent authorities shall perform an investigation to confirm or eliminate that suspicion (article 137 (2)). This might involve performing intensified official controls or the official detention of animals and goods (article 137 (3)).

This risk-based approach to enforcement is nothing new but has taken on a greater significance in recent times due to reduced funding for and lack of resources in some competent authorities.

Where following the investigation, non-compliance is established, competent authorities shall take:

1) any action necessary to determine the origin and extent of the non-compliance and to establish the operator's responsibilities; and

2) appropriate measures to ensure the operator concerned remedies the non-compliance and prevents further occurrences of such non-compliance

   (article 138 (1))

When deciding what measures to take, the competent authority is required to take account of the nature of the non-compliance and the operator's past record regarding compliance.

When non-compliance has been established, competent authorities are empowered to 'take any measure they deem appropriate to ensure compliance with the rules' and article 138 (2) provides a non-exhaustive list which includes:

i. restrict or prohibit the placing on the market, the movement, the entry into Great Britain or the export of animals and goods; and prohibit or order their return to the country of dispatch;

ii. order the recall, withdrawal, removal and detention of goods, authorising, where appropriate, the use of goods for purposes other than those for which they were originally intended;

iii. order the isolation or closure of all or part of the business of the operator concerned and, where relevant, the internet sites it operates or employs;

iv. order the suspension or withdrawal of the registration or approval of the establishment, plant or holding; and

v. order the slaughter or killing of animals where this is the most appropriate measure to safeguard human health and animal health and welfare.

Article 139 of the OCR refers to setting a level of penalties for breach of the Regulation that is 'effective, proportionate and dissuasive. The responsibility for doing so is placed on the 'appropriate authority'.

The appropriate authority is required to ensure that financial penalties for violations of the OCR perpetrated through fraudulent or deceptive practices reflect at least either the economic advantage for the operator, or as appropriate, a percentage of the operator's turnover.

The appropriate authority is defined in article 3 as:

a) in relation to England, the Secretary of State;

b) in relation to Wales, the Welsh Ministers;

c) in relation to Scotland, the Scottish Ministers;

The Secretary of State is the appropriate authority in respect of matters outside devolved competence or where consent has been given by the Welsh or Scottish Ministers as appropriate.

For the purposes of the OCR, the competent authority is defined in article 3 as the appropriate authority or the authority designated under article 4 and includes, where appropriate, the corresponding authority of a third country, of Northern Ireland or of any of the Crown Dependencies.

The 'Crown Dependencies' are the Bailiwick of Jersey, the Bailiwick of Guernsey and the Isle of Man.

Official controls – domestic law

National competent authorities include the Food Standards Agency, Food Standards Scotland, DEFRA, DAERA (Department of Agriculture, Environment and Rural Affairs) in Northern Ireland.

Responsibility for regulation and enforcement also falls on local authorities.

As noted above, it is necessary to check the relevant legislation to identify the correct competent authority, because only then can an assessment be made about whether the officer who carried out an action was properly authorised.

Food authorities are, generally speaking, local councils (see for example section 5 of the Food Safety Act 1990 as regards England, Wales and Scotland and the Food Safety (Northern Ireland) Order 1991.

Enforcement authorities

As with the correct identification of the competent authorities, regard must be had to the individual legislation to ascertain which authority has obligations for enforcement.

For example, for the purposes of the Food Safety Act 1990 and regulations made under it, every food authority shall 'enforce and execute within there are the provisions of the Act…' (section 6 Food Safety Act 1990).

Identifying the enforcement authority for the purposes of the Food Safety and Hygiene (England) Regulations 2013 is slightly more involved. Regulation 5 broadly delineates enforcement responsibility based on whether the food business operator operations are regulated under Regulation 852/2004 (the hygiene of food stuffs) or Regulation 853/2004 (specific hygiene rules for food of animal origin).

For food business operators whose operations are regulated by Regulation 852/2004 but not Regulation 853/2004, regulation 5 (1) of the 2013 regulations provides:

(a) the enforcement authority is either the Food Standards Agency or the relevant food authority, if the activities involved primary production and 'the transport, storage and handling of primary products at the place of production, provided that this does not substantially alter their nature'; and

(b) in respect of all other operations, the enforcement authority is the food authority in whose area the food business operator carries out those operations.

Where Regulation 852/2004 and Regulation 853/2004 apply, regulation 5 (2) of the 2013 regulations states that the enforcement authority is:

(a) the Food Standards Agency where the operations consist of a slaughterhouse, a game-handling establishment or a cutting plant;

(b) the Food Standards Agency or the food authority in whose are the food business operator carries out the operations.

Authorised Officers

On the ground enforcement of food law is undertaken by authorised officers (AO).

Although the terminology might change (e.g. the Welfare of Animals at the Time of Killing (England) Regulations 2015 refers to an 'inspector' – regulation 34), this chapter refers to all enforcement officials as AOs.

They are suitably qualified and experienced officials who have been authorised in writing, either generally or specifically, by the relevant authority to act in in matters specified in the legislation (see for example section 6 of the FSA 1990 and regulation 2 of the 2013 Regulations).

Legislation gives AOs two broad sets of powers; investigation powers (whether used as a consumer protection measure and/or as a precursor to enforcement action) and enforcement powers (e.g. to serve a statutory notice or commence a prosecution).

Whenever an official has undertaken an act which may only be carried out by an authorised officer, it is important to obtain proof that the person was authorised in respect of the act and that any authorisation was in force and valid at that time.

Investigation powers

It is always necessary to check the legislation in question to see what powers are given to an authorised officer.

Powers include:

1) Inspection and seizure of suspected food – section 9 (1) FSA 1990

Section 9 provides that an AO of a food authority may at all reasonable times inspect any food intended for human consumption which

(a) has been sold or is offered or exposed for sale;

(b) is in the possession of, or has been deposited with or consigned to, any person for the purpose of sale or of preparation for sale; or

(c) is otherwise placed on the market within the meaning of Regulation (EC) No. 178/2002.

It then provides the regime for dealing with food:

- 'where on such an inspection, it appears to the authorised officer that any food fails to comply with food safety requirements'; or

- 'where, otherwise than on such an inspection, it appears to an authorised officer of a food authority that any food is likely to cause food poisoning or any disease communicable to human beings'.

The AO may:

- give notice that the food is not to be used for human consumption and not removed (or removed to a specified place); or

- seize the food and have it dealt with by a justice of the peace and prescribed in section 9

Where the AO has served a notice, they must determine, 'as soon as reasonably practicable and in any event within 21 days' whether or not they are satisfied that the food complies with food safety requirements. If they are so satisfied, they must withdraw the notice 'forthwith' and if not, they must seize the food and have it dealt with by a justice of the peace.

If it appears to the justice of the peace on the basis of such evidence as they consider appropriate in the circumstances that the food fails to comply with food safety requirements, the food shall be condemned and destroyed or otherwise disposed of to prevent it entering the food chain and order that the owner of the food pays 'any expenses reasonably incurred in connection with the destruction or disposal' of the food.

If however the notice is withdrawn or the justice of the peace refuses to condemn the food, ' the food authority shall compensate the owner of the food for any depreciation in its value resulting from the action taken by the authorised officer.

2) Samples – e.g. section 29 FSA 1990

This section empowers an AO of an enforcement authority to -

- Purchase a sample of food or any substance capable of being used in the preparation of food.

- Take a sample of food or any such substance which –

'appears to him to be intended for sale, or to have been sold, for human consumption; or is found by him on or in any premises which he is authorised to enter by or under section 32 below'

- Take a sample for any food source or any contact material, which is found by them on those premises, and
- Take a sample 'of any article or substance which is found by him on or in any such premises and which he has reason to believe may be required as evidence in proceedings under any of the provisions of this Act or of regulations or orders made under it'.

Samples obtained pursuant to section 29 powers may submit it for analysis in accordance with the provisions of section 30 FSA 1990.

Regard should be had to the Food Safety (Sampling and Qualifications) (England) Regulations 2013 and the correct division of samples (regulations 14 and 15 of the Food Safety and Hygiene (England) Regulations 2013).

3) Entry – e.g. section 32 (1) FSA 1990

'An authorised officer of an enforcement authority shall, on producing, if so required, some duly authenticated document showing his authority, have a right at all reasonable hours—

(a) to enter any premises within the authority's area for the purpose of ascertaining whether there is or has been on the premises any contravention of the provisions of this Act, or of regulations or orders made under it; and

(b) to enter any business premises, whether within or outside the authority's area, for the purpose of ascertaining whether there is on the premises any evidence of any contravention within that area of any of such provisions; and

(c) in the case of an authorised officer of a food authority, to enter any premises for the purpose of the performance by the authority of their functions under this Act;

but admission to any premises used only as a private dwelling-house shall not be demanded as of right unless 24 hours' notice of the intended entry has been given to the occupier.'

Section 32 (2) of the 1990 Act provides for the application for a warrant to enter premises 'for any such purpose as is mentioned in subsection (1)'.

FBOs, and where applicable their advisers, should be aware of the AO's powers in the legislation applicable to them and should carefully check two documents; the 'duly authenticated document' (and record the identity of the AO) and the warrant. Problems with either could have significant adverse consequences for any enforcement action taken in reliance of them.

Enforcement powers

These are many and varied but include:

1) Improvement Notice – section 10 Food Safety Act 1990

   Where an authorised officer 'has reasonable grounds for believing that the proprietor of a food business is failing to comply with any regulations to which this section applies'

   Section 10 applies to regulations

   (a) for requiring, prohibiting or regulating the use of any process or treatment in the preparation of food; or

   (b) for securing the observance of hygienic conditions and practices in connection with the carrying out of commercial operations with respect to food or food sources.

2) Emergency prohibition notices and orders – regulation 8 Food Safety and Hygiene (England) Regulations 2013

Where an authorised officer 'is satisfied that the health risk condition is fulfilled with respect to any food business' they may serve a notice on the relevant food business operator imposing the 'appropriate prohibition'

The health risk condition – regulation 8 applying regulation 7 (2)

The health risk condition is fulfilled with respect to any food business if any of the following involves an imminent risk of injury to health (including any impairment, whether permanent or temporary), namely —

(a) the use for the purposes of the business of any process or treatment;

(b) the construction of any premises used for the purposes of the business, or the use for those purposes of any equipment; and

(c) the state or condition of any premises or equipment used for the purposes of the business.

The appropriate prohibition – regulation 8 applying regulation 7 (3)

(a) in a case falling within [regulation 7 (2) (a)] a prohibition on the use of the process or treatment for the purposes of the business;

(b) in a case falling within [regulation 7 (2) (b)] a prohibition on the use of the premises or equipment for the purposes of the business or any other food business of the same class or description; and

(c) in a case falling within [regulation 7 (2) (c)] a prohibition on the use of the premises or equipment for the purposes of any food business.

An application to the magistrates' court

Regulation 8 sets out several procedural matters relating to the service and display of the HEPN. It also requires the authorised officer to apply to the court for a Hygiene Emergency Prohibition Order and the court must either make the order if it is satisfied that the health risk condition is satisfied or, if the imminent risk of injury to health has been removed (for example by the food business operator having done works following the service of the HEPN), the court must declare itself satisfied that the health risk condition was fulfilled when the notice was served.

Failure to follow the specified procedure will result in the enforcement authority compensating the operator for any loss suffered by reason of complying with the notice (for example if the notice had the effect of closing the food business).

Enforcement – general provisions

Generally speaking, AO actions should be the least intrusive or least 'draconian' for the business as is justified in all the circumstances.

Enforcement action should be reasonable, proportionate, risk-based and consistent with good practice. As chapter 6 of the Food Law Code of Practice (England) June 2023 makes plain, it should also be in accordance with chapter 6 of the Food Law Practice Guidance (England) dated March 2021. Similar Codes and Guidance exist in the other UK nations.

When faced with actual or threatened enforcement action, FBOs and their advisers might find it helpful to consult the Code and the Guidance to 'sense-check' that the AO has followed the proper course.

Chapter 6 of the Food Law Code also makes clear that competent authorities and hence their AOs on the ground should have regard to a series of factors including the provisions of documents such as the Code for Crown Prosecutors, the Regulators' Code and, of course, their own enforcement policy.

Failure to have regard to those documents could leave the competent authority open to challenge, or at least sufficient criticism, as to 'force' them to reconsider their actions.

The competent authority and their AOs should always have regard to all relevant matters including the business's compliance history and attitude to the current alleged non-compliance. The enforcement approach may be different between a FBO who acknowledges their inadvertent or unintentional non-compliance and takes steps to rectify the situation and the FBO who has deliberately or negligently created a risk to public health and is reluctant or refuses to take appropriate action.

If the business has a Primary Authority Partnership in place, this will be a significant factor for the enforcement authority in determining how to procced.

The idea that actions should be the least intrusive or draconian is referred to as the hierarchy of enforcement. This is not an absolute rule in that the circumstances might justify the AO taking immediate official action, rather than for example issuing a warning to rectify or regularise the non-compliance.

The hierarchy of enforcement includes consideration of the following:

- the enforcement options – advice and education, sampling, detention of 'suspect' food, enforcement notices (HEPN, HIN, RAN etc,) and, finally criminal prosecution;

- moving from informal to formal action where the former has not achieved the desired aim where there is a significant risk to health or there are fraudulent or deceptive practices;
- resolving the non-compliance quickly and effectively; and
- prioritising action where there are risks to the health of humans, animals or plants or to animal welfare.

Ultimately, it is for the AO, often in consultation with senior colleagues, to decide what action is required and the onus falls on the food business operator to decide how to respond.

Conclusion

Food business operators and their staff should have a general understanding of who regulates their activities and the powers granted to the AOs (particularly around powers of entry and requests for assistance or to see documents).

They should also know how to respond to an official visit and to understand what the AO is looking for. First impressions really count in this type of situation. If the business makes a good impression in terms of the cleanliness and conditions and has all the necessary documents available for inspection, this will give the AO a degree of confidence in the business, its staff, its operations and its commitment to regulatory compliance and to consumer protection.

Of course, the opposite is true. A poor first impression can set the tone for the inspection that follows and can make official intervention more likely.

CHAPTER NINE

CHALLENGING ENFORCEMENT ACTION

Introduction

Faced with actual or threatened official action the food business operator (FBO) might understandably panic and be unclear about what is happening and what, if anything, they can or should do.

Sometimes, it will be necessary to comply with the authorised officer's (AO's) request. This might be informal or it might be included in an official enforcement notice.

Other occasions might require, and justify, the business operator pushing back and challenging, formally or informally, what the AO has asked them to do.

This chapter considers some of those responses and reviews the routes by which official enforcement action may be challenged.

One feature of dealing with AO action and intervention is the desire not to upset the officer or the competent authority and do whatever is necessary for a quiet life. Whilst this is perfectly understandable and might be the appropriate approach, the FBO might be correct to challenge what they are being asked to do.

The initial response

The first response will often be to check that the authority is the correct competent authority within the relevant legislation.

For example, regulation 4 of the Welfare of Animals at the Time of Killing (England) Regulations 2015 specifies that the Food Standards Agency is the competent authority for certain matters and the Secretary of State is the competent authority for other matters.

In the Scottish version of those regulations, the competent authority is either Food Standards Scotland or the Scottish Ministers.

In Wales it is the Food Standards Agency or the Welsh Ministers whereas in Northern Ireland, the competent authority is the Department of Agriculture and Rural Development.

Similarly, regulation 4 of the Food Safety and Hygiene (England) Regulations 2013 defines the competent authority as either the Food Standards Agency or a food authority.

The initial response may in part depend on the type of food business. For those that are approved (e.g. because they handle products of animal origin) they have regular, often daily, contact with the AO and might be able to find a resolution to the issue of concern before it becomes 'formal'.

For other food businesses that are only required to notify the competent authority that they are operating and have less, often much less, involvement and interaction with an AO, their response may be different.

The response of a small local food business might again be different to a large national or multi-national chain having ready access to in-house and external support.

However, the actions of the AO might have significant implications for the business in terms of time, resources and public relations, let alone the potential for court action due to challenging an enforcement action or defending a criminal prosecution.

Where possible, and it is not always possible due to the immediacy and/or timing of the official action, the FBO should take advice.

This might be informally within the business itself, for example consulting relevant managers or specialists such as quality control, or by contacting external sources such as the food consultant or legal adviser.

Regarding the latter option, going outside the business, one initial thought might be, 'what will this cost'. However, depending on the issue and the potential consequences, the financial cost of taking advice now may be very worthwhile and beneficial compared with what might follow.

Any notice served on the business should be carefully scrutinised for possible defects or avenues of challenge (whether formally or informally).

Taking time and thought at this stage and liaising with advisers will identify possible options to 'push back' on the AO's actions or will reveal that the legal and procedural issues relating to the action have been fulfilled.

Consideration will then be given to whether there are any challenges on the merits (e.g. is there an imminent risk to health for the service of a hygiene emergency prohibition notice – HEPN – regulation 8 of the 2013 Regulations) or does the food breach food safety requirements (seizure of food – section 9 FSA 1990).

Questioning the AO's actions

It may be possible to 'negotiate' an outcome that avoids formal action. This might mean offering to voluntarily close a food business to undertake remedial works such as cleaning overnight and asking the AO to return the following day. If conditions have improved, the imminent risk to health may no longer exist and an HEPN may not be necessary.

The AO and the competent authority should always be receptive to a point of view that differs from their own.

Of course, a busy and overstretched AO may be unable, or indeed unwilling, to accommodate such a request. If they have identified a risk to public health they may decide that anything other than issuing a formal notice may not be sufficient.

Challenging the AO's actions

Responding to enforcement action might be considered in three ways.

Legal and procedural challenges

- Is the official properly authorised?
- Has the AO strictly followed the statutory provisions?
- Does the notice comply with applicable section of the Act or regulation of the statutory instrument?
- Has the notice been served correctly?
- Does it meet the statutory requirements for its contents?
- Has the recipient been correctly identified and referenced in the notice (is the name of the company or individual correct)?

  Regarding the last point, it might be thought that the AO would name and serve the correct person. However, mistakes do happen.

  When the statutory provision empowers a notice to be served on the food business operator, the AO might have simply used the details on the registration or notification form, whereas the FBO might have changed (of course any change should have been notified to the competent authority). The FBO on the day might not be the one the AO believes is running the business.

Challenging the facts

- The FBO might argue that the conditions found in the premises or the condition of the food are not as the AO states or the situation is not so bad as the AO suggests.

  This might simply be a dispute of fact which the court will have to resolve. It might require the benefit of an expert opinion to assist the court as to the meaning of the legislative provision and whether the necessary conditions for the service notice are fulfilled having regard to the factual matrix.

  The expert may opine that the conditions do not give rise to an **imminent** risk of injury and hence the grounds for serving a HEPN are not met. However, the court only needs to be satisfied that the legal criteria are met and this low threshold is often met by the AO giving a brief explanation of what they saw and showing a series of photographs to the court!

Challenging the requisite 'mental requirement'

This is linked to the previous point

Prior to serving an enforcement notice, the AO is required to form a view based on the facts as they see or perceive them to be and apply them to the requisite state of mind as set out in the legislation. It may be possible to argue that the facts are insufficient to satisfy the mental requirement necessary to justify the service of the enforcement notice.

However, as public protection is paramount, the legislation does not place too onerous a burden on the AO, or indeed the court, regarding the justification for serving the notice.

- Section 9 FSA 1990 – inspection and seizure of food

  The criteria for further action are met **when it appears** to the AO that the food fails to comply with food safety requirements or the food is likely to cause food poisoning or any disease communicable to human beings

- Section 10 FSA 1990 – improvement notice

  The AO must have **reasonable grounds for believing** that the proprietor of a food business is failing to comply with any regulations to which this section applies …

  The notice must specify the measures which, **in the officer's opinion,** the proprietor must take to secure compliance;

- Regulation 8 Food Safety and Hygiene (England) Regulations 2013 – Hygiene Emergency Prohibition Notice

  Where AO **is satisfied** that the health risk condition is fulfilled …

- Regulation 38 (2) Welfare of Animals at the Time of Killing (England) Regulations 2015 – welfare enforcement notice

  An inspector who **is of the opinion** that …

Formally appealing the enforcement action/notice

In addition to informal challenges to the AO's actions being made within their competent authority, the recipient of an enforcement notice is usually, but always, given the power to appeal to a court or tribunal.

Whether an appeal is the correct approach depends on many factors, some of which have been discussed above.

Deciding on the next steps will have regard to some or all the following considerations:

- Is there a power to appeal or otherwise formally challenge the notice?

  The relevant legislation will specify whether a notice can be appealed and the notice should specify the appeal provisions.

  If so, is it an appeal as of right (e.g. statutory appeals to a court or tribunal) and what criteria need to be met, or is permission required (e.g. judicial review.

  Judicial review accompanied by an application for urgent injunctive relief might need to be considered where the legislation does not grant a power to appeal *The Queen on the application of Association of Independent Meat Suppliers v Food Standards Agency [2019] UKSC 36 and Case C-579/19*

- What is the venue for the appeal and what procedural steps are required?

  Is the appeal to the magistrates' court or the First-tier Tribunal?

  What paperwork is required and what is the time limit for submitting an appeal or otherwise challenging the notice?

- Once the appeal paperwork is lodged, how long before a final hearing will be heard and is there a power to stay or suspend the notice until that hearing?

  The court system and the tribunal system are under pressure and are not always geared up to hearing these types of appeals in a timely manner.

  Delay in fixing a final hearing could have a significantly detrimental effect on the recipient, its business and potentially the food in question. If the appeal cannot be heard promptly, it may be possible to apply for permission to bring a judicial review claim incorporating an injunction to protect the business's position pending a full hearing.

- More general considerations, at least for many businesses, are the time, cost and resource implications of pursuing an appeal. Even if all the other factors are balanced in favour of pursuing an appeal, these may be the deciding factors in deciding not to appeal and to spend the time, money and resources on complying with the notice.

  The business will have to pay its own legal and expert costs and, depending on the venue for the appeal, if it loses it may be ordered to pay the competent authority's costs.

The legislation used for the service of the enforcement notice will specify whether there are any appeal provisions and the notice itself will state the right of appeal, if any, and the time limit for bringing the appeal.

Appeals to the magistrates' court

Who may appeal?

For example, a person who 'is aggrieved by a decision' to serve an improvement notice under section 10 of the Food Safety Act 1990 may appeal to the magistrates' court (or in Scotland, to the sheriff) (section 37 (1) FSA 1990).

The procedure

An appeal comes within the court's civil jurisdiction and the appellant commences the appeal by way of complaint for an order (section 37 (3) FSA 1990), or in Scotland by summary application (section 37 (4) FSA 1990).

An appeal must be brought within one month from the date on which notice of the decision was served on the person desiring to appeal or in the case of an appeal under subsection (1)(a) above, that period or the period specified in the improvement notice, whichever ends the earlier (section 37 (5) FSA 1990).

The making of the complaint to the magistrates' court amounts to the bringing of the appeal (section 37 (5) FSA 1990).

As an appeal is by way of complaint for an order invoking the court's civil jurisdiction, Part II of the Magistrates Courts Act 1980 applies.

When considering an appeal against an improvement notice the court may either:

'cancel or affirm the notice and, if it affirms it, may do so either in its original form or with such modifications as the court may in the circumstances think fit.' (section 39 (1) FSA 1990).

Costs

The magistrates' court's civil jurisdiction to award costs is contained in section 64 (1) of the Magistrates' Courts Act 1980:

On the hearing of a complaint, a magistrates' court shall have power in its discretion to make such order as to costs—

(a) on making the order for which the complaint is made, to be paid by the defendant to the complainant;

(b) on dismissing the complaint, to be paid by the complainant to the defendant,

as it thinks just and reasonable.

Guidance on the application of the costs regime in these cases can be found in the following cases:

City of Bradford Metropolitan District Council v Booth [2000] 164 JP 485

Competition and Markets Authority (Respondent) v Flynn Pharma Ltd and another (Appellants) [2022] UKSC 14 and

The Commissioner of Police of the Metropolis and Idreess Malik and Ealing Magistrates' Court [2023] EWHC 3213 (Admin)

These and other cases should be considered but, for present purposes, the following core principles apply:

1) Costs do not necessarily follow the event – the loser does not automatically pay the winner's costs;

2) The magistrates' court has a discretion to make such order as it thinks just and reasonable. This applies to who should pay the costs (if any) and in what amount (if any);

3) Where a complainant has successfully challenged before justices an administrative decision made by a police or regulatory authority acting honestly, reasonably, properly and on grounds that reasonably appeared to be sound, in exercise of its public duty, the court should have regard to all the circumstances. These include the financial prejudice to the complainant and the need to encourage public authorities to make and stand by honest, reasonable and apparently sound administrative decisions made in the public interest without fear of exposure to undue financial prejudice if the decision is successfully challenged;

4) Although that might often result in the court making no order against the public authority, 'there is no generally applicable principle that all public bodies should enjoy a protected status as parties to litigation where they lose a case which they have brought or defended in the exercise of their public functions in the public interest.' (*Flynn Pharma Limited* at [97] per Lady Rose)

Further challenge

A further appeal may be made to the crown court by 'a person who is aggrieved' by the magistrates' court dismissal of the appeal (section 38 FSA 1990).

Appeals to the First-tier Tribunal

There has been a move to direct appeals away from the courts and into the tribunal system. Several food regulations provide that appeals against enforcement action lie to the First-tier Tribunal and not the magistrates' court.

Identifying when this alternative route of appeal applies is not always obvious and straightforward.

The Food Information Regulations 2014 (FIR 2014) provide an example of how the general appeal procedure applied in the Food Safety Act 1990.

The general rule is that the same basic principles apply but the references to the magistrates' court are replaced with the First-tier Tribunal.

The FSA 1990 as modified in the FIR 2014

1) Improvement notices – regulation 12 (1) states that section 10 (1) and (2) of the FSA 1990 apply to the FIR as modified by Part 1 of Schedule 4 of the FIR (the provisions of food information law that may result in the service of an improvement notice);

2) Appeals – regulation 12 (3) states that section 37 of the FSA 1990 applies to the FIR as modified by Part 3 of Schedule 4 of the FIR (a person aggrieved may appeal to the First-tier Tribunal);

3) Appeals against improvement notices – regulation 12 (4) states that section 39 of the FSA 1990 applies to the FIR as modified by

Part 4 of Schedule 4 of the FIR (the appeal is heard and determined by the First-tier Tribunal)

All other provisions of the FSA 1990 apply to an appeal to the FTT.

The First-tier Tribunal

The FTT is governed by the Tribunals, Courts and Enforcement Act 2007 and the Tribunal Procedure (First-tier Tribunal) (General Regulatory Chamber) Rules 2009, as amended.

It is probably fair to say that the procedure in the FTT is more regimented that in the magistrates' court.

1) The service of and contents of the notice of appeal are specified (rule 22);

2) The respondent's response to the notice of appeal (rule 23);

3) The appellant's reply to the respondent's response (rule 24);

4) Notice of hearings (rule 34);

5) The FTT's decision (rule 38);

6) Setting aside a decision which disposes of proceedings (rule 41);

7) Applications for permission to appeal from the FTT's decision (rule 42).

8) Section 11 of the 2007 Act states that, subject to specified exclusions, a person may appeal from the FTT to the Upper Tribunal but only where permission has been granted by the FTT or the UT.

   Applications must be made to the FTT first and if permission is refused the application is then made to the UT. Rather than deciding the application for permission 'on the papers', the UT might direct a 'rolled up' hearing in which the parties make full submissions and the UT then decided whether or not to grant permission and, if permission is granted, whether to allow the appeal.

9) The FTT may review its own decision in limited circumstances (rule 44)

Costs in the First-tier Tribunal

The tribunal is intended to enable individuals, who may not be legally represented, to seek redress in a variety of circumstances.

For present purposes, rule 10 states that the FTT may only make a costs order in two circumstances:

1) Under section 29 (4) of the 2007 Act and costs incurred in applying for such costs; and

2) if the Tribunal considers that a party has acted unreasonably in bringing, defending or conducting the proceedings.

This is a reasonably high bar for a person seeking their costs.

Section 29 (4) of the 2007 Act relates to 'wasted costs' defined in section 29 (5) as:

'any costs incurred by a party—

(a) as a result of any improper, unreasonable or negligent act or omission on the part of any legal or other representative or any employee of such a representative, or

(b) which, in the light of any such act or omission occurring after they were incurred, the relevant Tribunal considers it is unreasonable to expect that party to pay'

For an example of the FTT determining an appeal against the service of an improvement notice reference may be made to *Oydsea Limited v London Borough of Waltham Forest* [2024] UKFTT 157 (GRC) (the Honey (England) Regulations 2015 modifying the provisions of the FSA 1990 relating to improvement notices and appeals).

Conclusion

Responding to official action can be daunting for many food business operators. It can be easier to simply comply.

However, good decision-making involves knowing what powers the AO has and what powers the FBO is given to challenge the use of those powers. It also involves ensuring that the AO is requiring the FBO to take action that is legally required rather than an action that might be seen as 'a good idea'.

If the legislation provides for an appeal then it is important to be aware of any time limits that might apply to the appeal process and what procedure must be followed to start the appeal processes.

In the absence of a statutory power of appeal or where the issue is very urgent, the FBO may have no choice but to consider seeking permission to apply for a judicial review of the official action and to seek urgent relief to maintain the status quo pending a determination by the court or tribunal.

CHAPTER TEN

CRIMINAL PROSECUTIONS

Introduction

To dispel any possible myth that food law offences merely 'regulatory breaches' and not 'really criminal', regard may be had to the potential penalties that are available to the courts and the consequences of a food law conviction for organisations and, more particularly, for individuals.

Prosecutions for breaches of food law legislation must be conducted in accordance with general rules of criminal evidence and procedure and in compliance with the Criminal Procedure Rules.

Authorised officers may conduct interviews under caution with those they suspect are responsible for an alleged offence. While turning up to answer a few questions may seem innocuous, this stage of the process can be very significant in determining how the investigation proceeds.

Criminal prosecutions are usually, but not always, taken against the food business operator. It is therefore crucial for the competent authority to correctly identify this person; whether it is an organisation or an individual. One way of doing this is during an interview under caution.

Rather than attend in person to be interviewed, it is always possible to invite the competent authority to submit a list of questions which will be answered in writing under caution.

Whether the questions are answered in person or in writing, the consequences are so important that legal advice should be taken beforehand.

General criminal procedure and evidence

This is a complex area and a detailed review of the rules is outside the scope of this book.

However, the following brief selective summary may be useful.

The prosecution bears the burden of proof. It must prove the case to the requisite standard of beyond reasonable doubt or, put another way, so that the decision-maker is sure of the defendant's guilt on each summons or on each count of the indictment.

The defendant does not usually have to prove anything save in exceptional circumstances such as the defence of due diligence (see below).

The decision-maker on questions of guilt or innocence will be lay magistrates or a district judge in the magistrates' court or a jury in the crown court (the judge in the crown court deals with all matters of law).

Having conducted their investigation and obtained evidence to support the defendant's guilt, the authorised officers will submit their file to senior colleagues and the lawyers for review.

The decision to commence a criminal prosecution is taken having regard to the requirements of the Code for Crown Prosecutors (the Full Code Test) in the same way as all other criminal cases.

In essence, the decision-maker asks themselves two questions and must have a positive answer to each one:

1. Is there enough relevant, cogent and admissible evidence to provide a realistic prospect of conviction against each defendant on each alleged offence?

2. Is it in the public interest to bring a criminal prosecution?

Answering question 1 is often, but not always, relatively straightforward. There either is or there is not sufficient evidence.

If sufficient evidence exists, the competent authority must positively determine that the public interest requires a prosecution. This is not always as straightforward as question 1. There are many factors that might come into play and each case is fact specific. It is not possible to list all these factors but in a food law context, the following might be relevant:

1) The seriousness of the offence;

2) The culpability of the person(s) under investigation;

3) Was actual harm caused or what was the risk of harm to consumers;

4) The compliance history of the food business operator or person under investigation;

5) The attitude of the person under investigation. If the person readily accepted their failing, they have an otherwise good compliance history and took immediate remedial measures, in the absence of actual harm or a real risk of harm, it may, emphasis on may, tip the balance so that a prosecution is not necessary in the public interest;

6) In all the circumstances, is a prosecution a proportionate response. If other enforcement action has been taken that has remedied the default and protected consumers, it may, and again emphasis on may, tip the balance against prosecution.

It is important that competent authorities adopt the correct decision-making process before commencing a prosecution. Some of the public interest factors will often be raised by the person under investigation, for example during any interview under caution whether in person or in writing.

It is also important to check that the relevant official has the correct legal authority and/or has been properly delegated to commence the criminal prosecution.

Chapter 6 of both the Food Law Code and the Guidance deal with enforcement including criminal prosecutions and are worth consulting when advising a client.

Those chapters set out a series of matters that are relevant to the taking of enforcement action. These include the competent authority's own enforcement policy and whether a Primary Authority Partnership is in place.

Once the decision has been taken to prosecute, the authority must have regard to the applicable Criminal Procedure Rules. At this stage of the process, Part 7 'Starting a Prosecution in the Magistrates' Court' and Part 8 'Initial Details of the Prosecution Case' are particularly relevant.

Failure to comply with the Rules can lead to legal challenges (e.g. Part 7 was considered in *The King (on the Application of Chopstix Trading Limited) and Luton Magistrates' Court* [2022] EWHC 3141 (Admin) following the decision in *Food Standards Agency v Bakers of Nailsea Limited* [2020] EWHC 3632 (Admin)).

As an alternative to a criminal prosecution, the investigation may result in the person under investigation accepting a simple caution.

Food law offences

The legislation will clearly specify whether an act or omission gives rise to a criminal offence and will specify whether the offence may be only tried in the magistrates' court (summary offence) or may be tried in the magistrates' court or the crown court (either-way offence). The maximum penalties will be stated and the next chapter will look at how the court approaches the sentencing of food law cases.

Food Safety Act 1990

The Act contains many provisions which create criminal offences for example:

Section 7	Rendering food injurious to health (but see article 14 of Regulation 178/2002 – placing unsafe food on the market – which is used as an alternative to section 7);
Section 14	Selling food not of the nature or substance or quality demanded
Section 15	Falsely describing or presenting food
Section 15C	Duty to report non-compliance with food information law – Scotland only – see section 33 of the Food (Scotland) Act 2015

Food Safety and Hygiene (England) Regulations 2013

One of the more common offence creating provisions is found in regulation 19 (1) of the 2013 Regulations:

'Subject to paragraphs (4) to (9), any person who contravenes or fails to comply with any of the specified EU provisions commits an offence.'

The 'specified EU provisions' are set out in schedule 2 of the 2013 Regulations and include:

1) Placing unsafe food on the market (article 14 of Regulation 178/2002);

2) Failing to comply with traceability requirements (article 18 of Regulation 178/2002);

3) Failing to comply with obligations to notify competent authorities, undertake withdrawals and/or recalls when food fails to comply with food safety requirements (article 19 of Regulation 178/2002);

4) Failing to comply with the general hygiene requirements (article 4, Annex I and Annex II of Regulation 852/2004). These include some of the main hygiene obligations; keeping food premises clean, having adequate procedures in place to control pests, protecting food from contamination, personal hygiene and training;

5) Failing to comply with HACCP requirements (article 5 of Regulation 852/2004);

6) Failing to notify the competent authority about the operation of food business establishments (article 6 of Regulation 852/2004);

7) Failing to comply with the specific hygiene requirements for products of animal origin (article 3 of Regulation 853/2004); and

8) Failing to obtain approval if handling specified products of animal origin (article 4 of Regulation 853/2004).

Food legislation provides for the criminal prosecution of individuals as well as organisations.

An individual might be criminally liable for a breach of food law:

1) As the food business operator;

2) Where the offence may be committed by 'any person' (e.g. obstruction contrary to section 33 of the Food Safety Act 1990 or

regulation 17 of the Food Safety and Hygiene (England) Regulations 2013);

3) In their capacity as a representative of a company that has committed a food law offence.

In respect of the last point, food legislation frequently contains a provision headed 'offences by bodies corporate' which imposes criminal liability on individuals.

By way of example, section 36 (1) of the Food Safety Act 1990:

'Where an offence under this Act which has been committed by a body corporate is proved to have been committed with the consent or connivance of, or to be attributable to any neglect on the part of—

(a) any director, manager, secretary or other similar officer of the body corporate; or

(b) any person who was purporting to act in any such capacity,

he as well as the body corporate shall be deemed to be guilty of that offence and shall be liable to be proceeded against and punished accordingly.'

Although broad generalisations can be misleading, the following may be useful:

Consent – presupposes knowledge of the circumstances that led to the offence;

Connivance – implies knowledge of, and acquiescence in, the offence committed;

Neglect – a failure to perform a duty of which the individual knows or ought to know

Reference may also be made to section 36A of the Food Safety Act 1990 in respect of the individual liability in Scottish partnerships.

Section 36, and indeed section 36A, are one of a series of sections in the Food Safety Act 1990 that are incorporated into food regulations (e.g. the Food Information Regulations 2014).

Time limits

Food legislation sets out the time limit within which criminal proceedings must be commenced.

Most food law offences are 'either-way' offences which means that they may be tried in the magistrates' court or in the crown court.

In 'general' criminal law, some of these 'either-way' offences are not subject to time restrictions and so offences may be prosecuted years after they have been committed (for example health and safety offences).

Food law offences do not have that luxury and are often subject to time limits.

Offences which are summary only and can only be tried in the magistrates' court are subject to a limitation period of 6 months from the time the offence was committed.

One example of a summary only offence in food law is the offence of obstruction (see regulations 17 and 19 (3) of the Food Safety and Hygiene (England) Regulations 2013 and the equivalent in sections 33 and 35 (1) of the Food Safety Act 1990).

Other food law offences that are triable either way are usually subject to a longer time limit which is often expressed in terms similar to regulation 18 of the Food Safety and Hygiene (England) Regulations 2013:

> 'No prosecution for an offence under these Regulations which is punishable under paragraph (2) of regulation 19 shall be begun after the expiry of—
>
> (a) three years from the commission of the offence; or
>
> (b) one year from its discovery by the prosecutor,
>
> whichever is the earlier.'

A similar provision may be found in section 34 of the Food Safety Act 1990.

It is incumbent on authorised officers and competent authorities to ensure their investigation and decision-making are timely to avoid missing the deadline. It is equally important for defendants and their advisers to check that proceedings were commenced within the statutory time limit.

As noted above, reference should also be made to the provisions of Part 7 of the Criminal Procedure Rules, 'Starting a Prosecution in a Magistrates' Court' which sets out the requirements for a prosecutor who wishes the court to issue a summons.

Act or default of another person

Food law recognises that one person in the food chain might technically be guilty of an offence, but the 'real culprit' is someone else in the chain. In such circumstances, the authorised officer and the competent authority might 'by-pass' the first person and proceed against the second person.

For example, a food product on sale in retail premises does not comply with food information requirements. The person responsible for the information error is the manufacturer and they, rather than the retailer, are prosecuted.

'Where the commission by any person of an offence under any of the preceding provisions of this Part is due to an act or default of some other person, that other person shall be guilty of the offence; and a person may be charged with and convicted of the offence by virtue of this section whether or not proceedings are taken against the first-mentioned person.' (section 20 of the Food Safety Act 1990, and see regulation 11 of the Food Safety and Hygiene (England) Regulations 2013).

Strict liability

The main purposes of food law include the protection of consumers from harm and the protection of their interests. If the competent authority was required to prove that the food business operator intended to break the law then food law would become almost unenforceable.

Food law has therefore created strict liability offences in which the prosecution need only prove the act, or omission, has occurred (the *actus reus*), rather than having to also prove any intention or other mental element (the *mens rea*) to commit the offence.

Article 14 of Regulation 178/2002 states:

> 'Food shall not be placed on the market if it is unsafe'

If food is placed on the market and it is unsafe, this creates an offence under regulation 19 (1) of the Food Safety and Hygiene (England) Regulations 2013.

It would be much harder to prosecute a case in which it had to be proved that the business intended to place food on the market when they knew the food was unsafe. Consumer protection would be seriously undermined.

Very few food law offences require proof of *mens rea* and this will need to be proved by way of adducing in court sufficient admissible, relevant and cogent evidence (for example obtained during an interview under caution) obtained by the authorised officers during the investigation stage.

An example of an offence requiring proof of *mens rea* is obstruction:

> 'Any person who —
>
> (a) intentionally obstructs a person acting in the execution of the Hygiene Regulations or Regulation 178/2002;
>
> (b) …
>
> commits an offence.'

(Regulation 17 of the Food Safety and Hygiene (England) Regulations 2013; see also similar provisions in section 33 of the Food Safety Act 1990)

Due diligence – can the truly innocent avoid criminal liability?

As seen elsewhere in this book, food law non-compliance can be met with a variety of responses from the competent authority.

In an appropriate case, the non-compliance may result in civil proceedings, for example where consumers seek damages for the harm caused to them by unsafe food placed on the market. The standard of proof in such proceedings, on the balance of probabilities, is lower than in criminal proceedings.

Criminal food law recognises that non-compliances, even serious ones, can occur despite the business having put in place measures to prevent this happening.

In such circumstances, the defendant in criminal proceedings may rely on the defence of due diligence. There are too many nuances to this defence to list here so the following is a very brief overview of the defence, what it means and whether to deploy it or to plead guilty and present mitigation (the dividing line between a due diligence defence and mitigation is not always clear cut).

The defence:

> 'In any proceedings for an offence under any of the preceding provisions of this Part (in this section referred to as 'the relevant provision'), it shall, subject to subsection (5) below, be a defence for the person charged to prove that he took all reasonable precautions and exercised all due diligence to avoid the commission of the offence by himself or by a person under his control.'

(section 21 (1) of the Food Safety Act 1990 – other food legislation includes similar provisions, for example regulation 12 of the Food Safety and Hygiene (England) Regulations 2013)

As a preliminary point, it will be observed that the burden of proofing this defence moves to the defendant. This must be done to the civil standard of proof which, as just noted, is the balance of probabilities.

There are some procedural issues that must be complied with such as serving written notice on the prosecutor 'giving such information identifying or assisting in the identification of that other person as was then in his possession'.

There are two primary issues to consider. The defendant must prove that they:

1. Took all reasonable precautions; and

2. Exercised all due diligence

Applying a broad-brush approach to the meaning of both expressions, it may be considered that taking reasonable precautions equates to setting up an appropriate system within the food business and exercising due diligence might be thought of as ensuring that the system is working.

Allied to those requirements, the food business operator must maintain proactive vigilance of the system, review it regularly and if flaws are identified timely and effective remedial measures must be taken.

This is part of a positive food safety culture and/or a suitable food safety management system; reviewing what the business does, identifying where problems might occur, finding ways to prevent those problems materialising and guarding against complacency.

Some relevant matters to consider:

1. Each case must be assessed on its own merits. The defence is very fact specific to the offence and the business;

2. The business, meaning those in positions of seniority, must have done something positive to prevent the offence happening. There may be lots of measures in place, but are there measures in place that relate directly to the circumstances leading to the commission of the offence in question?

3. The identified measures will be assessed by reference to a variety of factors including – the size and resources of the business, the risk imposed by the products, whether the business carried out testing or whether they relied on assurances about compliance from others;

4. Are 'near-misses' or complaints properly recorded and reviewed to see if there is a pattern of problems with the system?

5. Where issues with the system have been raised or identified, have suitable and sufficient remedial measure been taken?

Having identified the measures that had been put in place, the business and its advisers need to consider whether those measures amount to mitigation, and possibly very good mitigation, or whether they afford the opportunity to pursue a due diligence defence.

These discussions will take place within the framework of all the facts and circumstances of the case.

If the due diligence is successful, the defendant will be acquitted.

If it is unsuccessful, the defendant will be convicted and upon sentence will not be entitled to any reduction in penalty.

If the defendant decides that all its investigations are better presented as good mitigation, they may plead guilty and receive an appropriate reduction in the ultimate penalty (discussed further in the next chapter).

Sometimes, an issue arises in which the food business attributes the commission of the offence to some of its employees; they did not do as they had been trained to do, they did something unexpected, they failed to follow the written processes and procedures relevant to the circumstances of the offence.

Blaming employees may not be seen as an endearing quality in a defendant, but there may be occasions where the business believes it could have done no more to ensure that it and its staff did not commit the offence in question.

However, the business must accept that human error sometimes occurs because of some system error (e.g. lack of training, understanding or supervision) and blaming the individual might highlight failings in the system.

Pursuing a due diligence defence will entail the business relying on written evidence of policies, procedures and systems that existed at the time of the offence (e.g. cleaning schedules or cooking/cooling records were being completed properly and this was being checked by supervisors).

Businesses and advisers can go through these documents and decide whether they can reasonably form the basis of a due diligence defence.

However, the defendant will also need to present 'live' evidence through witnesses at trial. While the documents almost speak for themselves, there is a lot more uncertainty when witnesses go into the witness box and are cross-examined.

Finally, defendants can consider due diligence in the context of 'bites of the cherry'.

They can accept that the offence is proved and rely solely on due diligence (one bite) or they can argue that the offence is not made out, or to be more accurate at trial the prosecution cannot and does not prove its case and if it does, the defendant then relies on the due diligence defence (two bites).

Conclusion

The consequences of a criminal conviction are serious for a company but are particularly serious for an individual (they are a convicted criminal and this may need to be disclosed in certain circumstances).

As food offences are mainly strict liability, it may be thought that they are impossible to defend. Whilst they may not always be easy to defend, this does not mean that in the appropriate case, a full and robust defence can and should be deployed.

In addition to legal reasons for not defending a criminal prosecution, the next chapter reveals that there may also be commercial and financial reasons why a criminal prosecution concludes with a guilty plea.

CHAPTER ELEVEN

SENTENCING

Introduction

Many food law offences fall to be sentenced in line with the Health and Safety Offences, Corporate Manslaughter and Food Safety and Hygiene Offences Definitive Guideline ('the Sentencing Guideline').

As will be explained in more detail below, the Guideline provides an indication of the range of penalties (fines and imprisonment) available to the sentencing court. The two main issues that affect sentencing are culpability and harm (actual harm or likelihood of harm).

When first instructed to defend a food law prosecution brought against an organisation, the financial position will provide an early indication of the potential size of the fine. Although no defendant should plead guilty when they have a defence, another consideration when advising an organisation, particularly a large or very large one, is the credit to be given for an early guilty plea which can have a significant impact on the overall financial penalty.

Depending on the circumstances of the offence and the defendant, preparation for the sentencing exercise can be complex and requires a significant input in terms of resources from the client and their advisers. Experience tends to show that the effort put in in advance of the court hearing can reap significant rewards in obtaining an optimal result for the food business.

The prosecution has an important role to play in presenting the evidence to assist the court assess culpability and harm. The focus on this chapter will be on preparation for the sentencing hearing on behalf of the defendant.

The Sentencing Guideline – legal basis

The Sentencing Guideline ('the Guideline') was issued in accordance with section 120 of the Coroners and Justice Act 2009 and applied to all cases sentenced on or after 1 February 2016.

When sentencing breaches of specified food law, the court must follow the Guideline 'unless the court is satisfied that it would be contrary to the interests of justice to do so' (section 59 (1) of the Sentencing Code).

The Guideline consists of a series of categories containing a starting point sentence and a range of sentences to reflect the different levels of seriousness (i.e. based on the assessment of culpability and harm).

Credit for guilty pleas is then factored into the sentence as the court works through the Guideline's step-by-step approach.

The Sentencing Guideline – general commentary

The Guideline applies to the sentencing of food law offences committed under regulation 19 (1) of the Food Safety and Hygiene (England) Regulations 2013. In Wales, the Guideline applies to offences committed under regulation 17 (1) of the Food Hygiene (Wales) Regulations 2006 and the General Food Regulations 2004.

These offences relate to breaching various assimilated (EU) legislative provisions. For food law offences not covered by the Guideline, the parties and the court will have regard to its contents as it reflects the general approach to the sentencing of criminal offences.

As the magistrates' court has the power to impose unlimited fines, most cases involving organisations are finalised in that court, rather than being sent to the crown court.

However, the position is different for the sentencing of individuals as the magistrates' court does not generally have the power to impose a custodial sentence for food law offences (save for an offence under regulation 4 of the General Food Law Regulations 2004 in Wales where the magistrates' court can impose term of imprisonment of up to six months).

One example where the magistrates' court is empowered to impose a custodial sentence is in relation to obstruction offences where that court may impose a maximum term of three months in custody and/or a fine (e.g. regulation 19 (3) Food Safety and Hygiene (England) Regulations 2013, regulation 17 (3) Food Hygiene (Wales) Regulations 2006 and section 35 (1) food Safety Act 1990).

When sentencing an individual for an offence covered by the Guideline, if the magistrates' court thinks that the offence is so serious that it reaches the custody threshold indicated in the Guideline, it will (subject to the exception in the 2004 Regulations just mentioned) commit the matter to the crown court for sentence. A pre-sentence report will be required and on the day of sentencing the individual will be expected to go into the dock during the hearing and be subject to the same treatment as other defendants appearing in court.

The Guideline – practical application

Most sentencing hearings for food law offences will follow the prosecution having served an opening note/sentencing note to which the defendant will reply. These documents will be served on the court, with any supporting documentation in advance thus enabling the magistrates or district judge (or judge in the crown court) to understand the basic facts of case and any specific issues.

Regrettably, the sentencing documents do not always reach the magistrates or judge before the hearing. Fortunately, most do and so the parties can present their respective cases to a court having some familiarity with the facts and issues.

The parties may have agreed in advance certain issues such as culpability and harm, but the final decision on all sentencing matters remains with the court.

The Guideline provides a structure for the parties and the court but it retains sufficiently flexible to allow the court to have regard to all relevant matters (for example see the comments at paragraph 12 of *Whirlpool Appliances v Regina (HSE) [2017]* EWCA Crim 2186, as applied for example in *R (HSE) v ATE Truck and Trailer Sales Limited* [2018] EWCA Crim 752).

Sentencing organisations

<u>Step One – Determining the offence category</u>

The court does this by assessing the defendant's culpability and the harm caused, or risk of harm created, by the offence(s). Risk of harm follows the usual risk assessment of the likelihood of harm occurring and the extent of it if it does.

Culpability

• Very high

Deliberate breach of or flagrant disregard for the law

• High

Offender fell far short of the appropriate standard; for example, by:

- failing to put in place measures that are recognised standards in the industry
- ignoring concerns raised by regulators, employees or others

- allowing breaches to subsist over a long period of time

Serious and/or systemic failure within the organisation to address risks to health and safety

• Medium

Offender fell short of the appropriate standard in a manner that falls between descriptions in 'high' and 'low' culpability categories

Systems were in placc but these were not sufficiently adhered to or implemented

• Low

Offender did not fall far short of the appropriate standard; for example, because:

- significant efforts were made to secure food safety although they were inadequate on this occasion

- there was no warning/circumstance indicating a risk to food safety

Failings were minor and occurred as an isolated incident

It is probably rare to encounter a finding of very high culpability.

It is not always straightforward to determine whether the organisation fell **far** short of the appropriate standard or merely fell short of it (high v medium culpability), having of course established what the appropriate standard is in the circumstances.

It will be highly relevant if the organisation can direct the court to its policies, procedures and systems in place to prevent the offence and explain why and how they failed on the date in question. So, these issues are not only relevant to whether the organisation can consider pursuing a due diligence defence, they may have a significant impact on the court's assessment of culpability.

Harm

Category 1	• Serious adverse effect(s) on individual(s) and/or having a widespread impact
	• High risk of an adverse effect on individual(s) including where supply was to groups that are vulnerable
Category 2	• Adverse effect on individual(s) (not amounting to Category 1)
	• Medium risk of an adverse effect on individual(s) or low risk of serious adverse effect
	• Regulator and/or legitimate industry substantially undermined by offender's activities
	• Relevant authorities unable to trace products in order to investigate risks to health, or are otherwise inhibited in identifying or addressing risks to health
	• Consumer misled regarding food's compliance with religious or personal beliefs
Category 3	• Low risk of an adverse effect on individual(s)
	• Public misled about the specific food consumed, but little or no risk of actual adverse effect on individual(s)

In the absence of actual harm, for example illness caused by unsafe food, assessing risk of harm can be tricky. It may be necessary to engage an expert with suitable experience and expertise to assist the court make an assessment (the expert's role being to assist the court not to push the agenda of the party instructing them).

This may be particularly important in cases involving pests where there is potential for contamination of food to the extent that it becomes a potential health concern (e.g. Regulation 852/2004, Annex II Chapter IX, paragraphs 3 and 4)

Factors having a potential impact here include the type of foods (packaged or loose) being made or available to purchase, the activities in the food premises (manufacturing, producing or simply retailing packaged products) and whether a consumer had purchased and/or consumed contaminated food.

Step Two – Starting point and category range

The court is now interested in the financial position of the organisation. This will be identified in the form of accounts or similar financial documents covering a period that will reflect the true position, taking account of fluctuations in fortune (presenting three years' accounts or equivalent is often sufficient).

At step two, the court will be interested in the annual turnover figure; other matters such as profitability will be considered at step three.

The court should only have regard to the financial figures for the organisation that stands to be sentenced unless, as the Guideline observes, 'exceptionally it is demonstrated to the court that the resources of a linked organisation are available and can properly be taken into account'. This point may be seen in *Regina v Tata Steel UK Limited* [2017] EWCA Crim 704.

The turnover figure determines the category in which the organisation now will be sentenced.

There are four categories:

1. Large – turnover or equivalent – £50 million and over

2. Medium – turnover or equivalent – between £10 million and £50 million

3. Small – turnover or equivalent – between £2 million and £10 million

4. Micro – turnover or equivalent – not more than £2 million

There is a fifth, informal category, of a very large organisation (VLO) where the organisation's turnover or equivalent 'very greatly exceeds the threshold for large organisations'. Here, the court may find it necessary to move outside the suggested range to achieve a proportionate sentence.

In 2024, the Sentencing Council published a consultation document proposing amendments to selected sentencing guidelines. The consultation includes proposals for sentencing VLOs by amending the Guideline. It will be important to see what effect, if any, this has on the sentencing exercise for these organisations.

There is no magic figure above which an organisation should be classed as a VLO.

Each of the four Guideline categories contains a table setting out the starting point fine based on the court's assessment of culpability and harm. For each starting point fine there is a range that enables the court to take into account factors that increase seriousness, or which reduce seriousness or provide mitigation.

It is not possible here to show the figures for all categories but one example involving a large organisation is:

High culpability	Starting Point	Range
Harm category 1	£500,000	£200,000 – £1,400,000
Harm category 2	£230,000	£90,000 – £600,000
Harm category 3	£90,000	£50,000 – £240,000

The Guideline then provides a non-exhaustive list of factors that may permit the court to move up or down the range, or even on occasion to move outside the range.

Factors affecting seriousness

The court must be careful to avoid double counting any factors that it has already taken into account when assessing culpability and/or harm.

1. Relevant previous convictions
2. Motivated by financial gain
3. Deliberately concealing the illegal nature of the activity
4. Evidence of a wider or community impact
5. Breach of any court order
6. Obstruction of justice
7. Poor food safety or hygiene record
8. Refusal of free advice or training

Factors reducing seriousness or reflecting mitigation

1. No relevant previous convictions
2. Steps taken to voluntarily remedy the problem
3. High level of cooperation with the investigation, beyond that which will always be expected
4. Good food safety or hygiene record
5. Self-reporting, co-operation and acceptance of responsibility

<u>Step Three – Check whether the proposed fine based on turnover is proportionate to the overall means of the offender</u>

At steps three and four, the court is required to 'step back' and, where necessary, to adjust its initial fine to ensure it fulfils the objectives of sentencing.

The fine should meet, in a fair and proportionate way, the objectives of punishment, deterrence and the removal of gain derived through the commission of the offence; it should not be cheaper to offend than to take the appropriate precautions.

The court is now also asked to ensure that the fine is sufficiently substantial to have a real economic impact which will bring home to both management and shareholders the need to operate within the law.

This is a clear message to the organisation being sentenced, and as a deterrent to other food businesses, that any fine will impact individuals as well as the organisation in a clear attempt to affect change in behaviour and attitude.

The court will also have regard to whether the organisation is profitable or is loss-making and whether any financial benefit can be derived from the offence, for example by avoiding costs that would have been necessary to ensure compliance.

The court may also interrogate the accounts to see how much the directors are paid and use that figure in its calculations.

Step Four – Consider other factors that may warrant adjustment of the proposed fine

Where the organisation is a public or charitable body, the court will have regard to the impact of the fine on the provision of services, on the employment of staff or the local economy (but not the impact on directors and shareholders).

The onus will be on the organisation to put before the court evidence of the impact of a fine. Although the actual level of fine will not be known until the hearing, by working its way through the Guideline, the organisation will be able to identify the potential impact of the estimated fine or range of fines.

Step Five – Consider any factors which indicate a reduction, such as assistance to the prosecution

As organisations are always required to assist the investigating officers, step five is unlikely to apply in the routine case.

However, it might apply where the organisation, through its human actors, has provided significant information that has helped the investigators trace others who have played a major part in the illegal activity (e.g. identifying the ring-leaders of large-scale criminal activity – potentially in a large food crime case).

Step Six – Reduction for guilty pleas

As noted elsewhere, this can play a significant part in the initial discussions about how the organisation should respond to the prosecution case. For a large, or very large, organisation, the reduction at step six may reduce the overall fine considerably.

Reference may be made to the 'Reduction in sentence for a guilty plea guideline' for a detailed application of the principle.

The court will consider reducing its proposed fine by one-third where the guilty plea was entered a very early stage in the proceedings (usually the first hearing at which the court seeks a plea or indication of plea).

Guilty pleas entered after that stage will usually receive a reduction but this will be less than one-third and is likely to range from between one-quarter to one-tenth where the plea is entered at trial.

The court will have regard to the above and all the circumstances and may decide that a guilty plea should receive no reduction. However, as a guilty plea, whenever entered, avoids witnesses having to give evidence and saves time and cost, it would be reasonable to expect some reduction.

<u>Step Seven – Compensation and ancillary orders</u>

At this step, the court may award compensation to the victims of the offence. In food cases this is unusual in that there are rarely identifiable victims, the offence often concerning risk of harm to consumers.

In the situation where a consumer alleges that they have suffered injury, for example they were made ill through eating unsafe food, they are most likely to seek compensation outside of the criminal court system.

The court may also consider imposing a Hygiene Prohibition Order which has the effect of prohibiting the use of any process, treatment, premises or equipment (see regulation 7 of the Food Safety and Hygiene (England) Regulations 2013 and regulation 7 of the Food Hygiene (Wales) Regulations 2006).

Step Eight – Totality principle

The court must have regard to the overall fine having regard to the number of guilty pleas. It is not simply a case of setting a fine of X in respect of one offence and multiplying it by the number of offences, although the court may announce its sentence in that way so long as it has considered the impact of the total fine.

On other occasions, the court may select one offence as being the most serious and impose the fine for that offence and impose no separate penalty in respect of the other offences.

Those considerations tend to apply when the court is dealing with similar offences committed on the same day at the same premises. For example, the environmental health officer's inspection of the food business results in several offences for breaches of the hygiene legislation.

If there are several hygiene offences and a food safety case relating to unsafe food, the court might impose one fine for the hygiene offences but impose an additional fine for the safety offence.

If the court is sentencing for offences committed on separate days, then it is likely to impose separate fines for each day in the form of consecutive sentences.

However the court approaches the sentencing exercise, the total fine must be one that is just and appropriate in all the circumstances of the offence(s) and the offender.

Step Nine – Reasons

The court must give reasons for, and explain the effect of, the sentence.

It is only now that the organisation and its lawyers will know the starting point fine, the court's reasons for moving up or down the range and whether it then varied the sentence.

At this stage, the organisation may need to clarify the explanation of the sentence to be clear about the starting point sentence and any variations to see if the court has applied the Guideline correctly.

Sentencing individuals

An individual might be sentenced as the food business operator or because they the offence may be committed by any person or in their capacity as a:

- director, manager, secretary or other similar officer of the body corporate; or
- any person who was purporting to act in any such capacity

(e.g. regulation 20 Food Safey and Hygiene (England) Regulations 2013 and regulation 18 of the Food Hygiene (Wales) Regulations 2006).

The Sentencing Guideline approaches the sentencing of individuals in a similar step-by-step approach to the sentencing of organisations. As such, it is unnecessary to provide as detailed account of the Guideline in operation as was done for organisations.

Apart from the individual having a criminal record, the most important feature of the sentencing process is the potential for a custodial sentence (in the crown court of up to two years and in the magistrates' court only in relation to the Food Regulations 2004 in Wales).

Step One – Determining the offence category

The court must assess the offender's culpability and actual harm cause or the risk of harm being caused.

Culpability

There are four categories:

• Very high

Where the offender intentionally breached, or flagrantly disregarded, the law

• High

Actual foresight of, or wilful blindness to, risk of offending but risk nevertheless taken

• Medium

Offence committed through act or omission which a person exercising reasonable care would not commit

• Low

Offence committed with little fault, for example, because:

- significant efforts were made to address the risk although they were inadequate on this occasion
- there was no warning/circumstance indicating a risk to food safety
- failings were minor and occurred as an isolated incident

There is some similarity here with the three categories of offending for directors and similar officers; consent, connivance and neglect. When considering whether to plead guilty to any offences, it is important to be clear which of these is being accepted by the individual, and indeed which is being alleged by the prosecution.

Harm

Again the court is considering actual harm or the risk of harm (likelihood of harm occurring and the extent of it if it does).

Category 1	Serious adverse effect(s) on individual(s) and/or having a widespread impact High risk of an adverse effect on individual(s) – including where supply was to persons that are vulnerable
Category 2	Adverse effect on individual(s) (not amounting to Category 1) Medium risk of an adverse effect on individual(s) or low risk of serious adverse effect Regulator and/or legitimate industry substantially undermined by offender's activities Relevant authorities unable to trace products in order to investigate risks to health, or are otherwise inhibited in identifying or addressing risks to health Consumer misled regarding food's compliance with religious or personal beliefs
Category 3	Low risk of an adverse effect on individual(s) Public misled about the specific food consumed, but little or no risk of actual adverse effect on individual(s)

Step Two – Starting point and range

Having established the offence category, the court must consider what disposal options are available and in what circumstances should they be considered.

The court will need to be provided with the individual's financial information. This will usually be done by completing a means form, but this information may also be available from any Pre-Sentence Report.

Custody becomes a potential sentence where the court assesses the case to be high culpability with harm in category 2. The range for such an offence is a Band D fine to 26 weeks' custody.

Where the range includes custody, the court should consider:

- has the custody threshold been passed?
- if so, is it unavoidable that a custodial sentence be imposed?
- if so, can that sentence be suspended?

Where the range includes a community order, the court should consider whether the community threshold has been passed. Even if it has, a fine will usually be the most appropriate disposal.

The starting point sentence and range of sentences include a conditional discharge (the bottom of the range for low culpability and harm category 3) to a fine (within every range of sentences) to custody (9 months as a starting point for very high culpability and harm category 1 and within the ranges of other categories of offence).

The calculation of fines is based on a banding system as a percentage of relevant weekly income (RWI).

	Starting point	Range
Fine Band A	50% of RWI	25 – 75% of RWI
Fine Band B	100% of RWI	75 – 125% of RWI
Fine Band C	150% of RWI	125 – 175% of RWI
Fine Band D	250% of RWI	200 – 300% of RWI
Fine Band E	400% of RWI	300 – 500% of RWI
Fine Band F	600% of RWI	500 – 700% of RWI

As with organisations, the court is directed to a non-exhaustive list of factors that might require movement from the starting point fine within the range.

Factors increasing seriousness

1. Relevant previous convictions
2. Offence committed whilst on bail
3. Similar factors as for organisations including – motivated by financial gain, poor food safety or hygiene record, refusal of free advice and training

Factors reducing seriousness or reflecting personal mitigation

1. Similar factors as for organisations including – no relevant previous convictions, good food safety and hygiene record
2. A list of matters that might be relevant to the individual – positive character/exemplary conduct, mental disorder, serious medical condition, age and/or lack of maturity, sole primary carer for dependents, pregnancy, childbirth and post-natal care, difficult or

deprived background and prospects of work, training or education.

Step Three – Review and financial elements of the sentence

The court adopts the approach for organisations in that it takes a step back to review whether the sentence as a whole meets the objectives of sentencing (see above in relation to organisations).

Step Four – Consider any factors which indicate a reduction, such as assistance to the prosecution

This is unlikely to apply but see above in respect of organisations as to when it might be applicable (assistance leading to the identification of ring-leaders involved in food crime).

Step Five – Reduction for guilty pleas

The court will have regard to the guilty plea guideline (see in respect of organisations) and an early guilty plea should be 'rewarded' with a reduction of one-third off the proposed sentence.

Step Six – Compensation and ancillary orders

The conviction itself will have a significant impact on the individual.

The court may consider an award of compensation but for reasons set out above in respect of organisations, this may not be made.

Other orders include a Hygiene Prohibition Order or a director's disqualification order.

Step Seven -Totality principle

See above in relation to organisations

Step Eight – Reasons

The court has a duty to give reasons for, and explain the effect of, the sentence.

Conclusion

Preparation for a sentencing hearing following a guilty plea can involve substantial time and resources, and indeed a significant cost outlay. Whether that is justified very much depends on the case and the defendant's circumstances.

The time and expenditure on preparing for a hearing might be seen to be well worth it having regard to the significant impact that culpability and harm can have to the starting point penalty and the range of penalties that the court can impose.

In the absence of agreement on culpability and harm, the defence may need to instruct an expert or experts to assist the court with those issues.

CHAPTER TWELVE

OVERALL CONCLUSION AND THE FUTURE OF FOOD LAW IN THE UK

Despite what friends, family and some colleagues might think, food law is never boring!

The law is constantly changing in response to developments in science, technology, politics or policy, or simply to bring legislation up to date.

A small selection of recent changes includes:

- The introduction of additional checks on imported food products as set out in the Border Target Operating Model;
- Updated EU guidance on Novel Foods with the UK looking to streamline its own Novel Foods procedures;
- New UK legislation to enable nutrition and health claims law to be enforced by improvement notices and not just by criminal prosecution;
- New guidance from the Food Standards Agency and Food Standards Scotland on caffeine in food supplements;
- Changes to the list of allergens in Annex II to Regulation 1169/2011 on the Provision of Food Information to Consumers (EU not UK)

What about the future?

- Might there be a closer relationship between the UK and the EU? The recent UK general election (July 2024) saw the Labour Party take power with an agenda to review and reset the relationship?

- Might there be a new SPS (sanitary and phytosanitary) agreement in which UK officials undertake audits of EU plants with the aim of reducing the paperwork and bureaucracy, and cost, of importing foodstuffs into the UK while maintaining a high level of consumer protection?

- How will climate change affect food production, food security and food sustainability? Will developments in gene editing and genetic modification assist in this regard or will the inherent, in some quarters, suspicion and fear of such technology prevent this?

- Will the plant-based diet 'revolution' continue? Will there be a ban on meat names for plant-based foods?

- How will alternative protein sources, such as insects, be regulated and will this expand to cover more foodstuffs?

- How will Artificial Intelligence affect food systems, the food supply chain and detect pathogens in food production reducing the risk of unsafe food being a risk to consumers? Like many 'new' technologies, will AI become affordable in most, if not all food businesses?

- How will food systems cope with the next 'Covid-19'?

Despite all the advances in science, technology and processes, consumers still want the same thing. The food we eat must be safe, as described, affordable and available. Consumers want to make informed choices that meet their needs.

It is therefore incumbent on all food business operators wherever they sit in the food supply chain to understand their legal and moral obligations and follow them to the letter. Applying the basic rules including, cleanliness, avoiding contamination, openness, transparency and honesty will go a long way to achieve this.

Food law will continue to develop but the fundamentals of food law for businesses and consumers will remain the same.

Whatever your reasons for choosing to purchase this book, or to read some else's copy, you have done so because you have an interest in food law. You therefore have the power to affect future food laws, food regulations and food policy.

This might be in a small way by responding to consultations or a bigger way by developing or creating a product or system that helps to keep consumers safe or maintains food security or promotes a sustainable future.

Even food lawyers can play a positive role! This might be by assisting a client bring a new product to market, or to enter a brand-new market, or to help them develop a compliant label or marketing campaign that promotes the product in a legal and ethical manner.

When food businesses are subjected to enforcement proceedings, the food lawyer can assist manage the process and attempt a negotiated resolution. In criminal prosecutions the food lawyer can assist the business decide how to proceed and at court seek to persuade a judge that they do not need to impose a penalty that may ruin an otherwise hardworking and generally compliant food business or individual.

When acting for the competent authority, the food lawyer works in tandem with the Authorised Officers to present the evidence in a fair way enabling the judge to understand and assess the key issues and then make decisions accordingly.

Everyone involved in food production, supply, regulation, enforcement, legislation, policy and the final consumer has an important part to play in ensuring the UK's food system is and continues to be, fit for purpose.

MORE BOOKS BY LAW BRIEF PUBLISHING

A selection of our other titles available now:-

'A Practical Guide to Probation Breaches and Other Applications' by Mark Thomas
'A Practical Guide to Remarriage and Divorce' by Cordelia Williams & Claire Howard
'A Practical Guide to Privacy, Transparency, Reporting Restrictions and Closed Proceedings in the Court of Protection' by Laura Mannering
'Beaumont on Barristers – A Guide to Defending Disciplinary Proceedings (Second Edition)' by Marc Beaumont
'A Practical Guide to Payments for Environmental Services' by Ben Sharples
'A Practical Guide to the Law of Pregnancy and Maternity at Work' by Rebecca Thomas
'A Practical Guide to Redundancy – Second Edition' by Philip Hyland & Collette Moore
'A Practical Guide to International Issues for Scottish Family Lawyers' by Susie Mountain, Donna McKay, Ken MacDonald
'A Practical Guide to the Law on Deprivation of Liberty' by Ben Troke
'A Practical Guide to Rights over Airspace and Subsoil – Second Edition' by Daniel Gatty
'A Practical Guide to the Law in Relation to Inquests' by Ramya Nagesh
'A Practical Guide to the Construction and Rectification of Wills and Trust Instruments (Second Edition)' by Edward Hewitt
'A Practical Guide to Data Protection in Social Housing' by Clare Paterson
'A Practical Guide to Spousal Maintenance – Second Edition' by Liz Cowell
'A Practical Guide to International Parental Child Abduction Law (England and Wales)' by Dr Onyója Momoh
'A Practical Guide to Deprivation of British Citizenship' by Sean Ell
'A Practical Guide to Commercial Property Service Charges' by Rachel Garton
'A Practical Guide to Clinical Negligence – Third Edition' by Geoffrey Simpson-Scott (Geoff)
'A Practical Guide to the Rights of Grandparents in Children Proceedings – Second Edition' by Stuart Barlow

'The Electronic Communications Code: A Practical Guide – Second Edition' by Kerry Bretherton KC, James Castle, Mark Loveday

'A Practical Guide to the Independent School Standards – September 2023 Edition' by Sarah McKimm

'A Practical Guide to Estate Administration and Crypto Assets' by Richard Marshall

'A Practical Guide to Parental Alienation in Private and Public Law Children Cases' by Sam King QC & Frankie Shama

'Contested Heritage – Removing Art from Land and Historic Buildings' by Richard Harwood QC, Catherine Dobson, David Sawtell

'The Limits of Separate Legal Personality: When Those Running a Company Can Be Held Personally Liable for Losses Caused to Third Parties Outside of the Company' by Dr Mike Wilkinson

'A Practical Guide to Transgender Law' by Robin Moira White & Nicola Newbegin

'A Practical Guide to 'Stranded Spouses' in Family Law' by Mani Singh Basi

'A Practical Guide to Residential Freehold Conveyancing' by Lorraine Richardson

'A Practical Guide to Pensions on Divorce for Lawyers' by Bryan Scant

'A Practical Guide to Challenging Sham Marriage Allegations in Immigration Law' by Priya Solanki

'A Practical Guide to Digital Communications Evidence in Criminal Law' by Sam Willis

'A Practical Guide to Legal Rights in Scotland' by Sarah-Jane Macdonald

'A Practical Guide to New Build Conveyancing' by Paul Sams & Rebecca East

'A Practical Guide to Inherited Wealth on Divorce' by Hayley Trim

'A Practical Guide to Practice Direction 12J and Domestic Abuse in Private Law Children Proceedings' by Rebecca Cross & Malvika Jaganmohan

'A Practical Guide to Confiscation and Restraint' by Narita Bahra QC, John Carl Townsend, David Winch

'A Practical Guide to the Law of Forests in Scotland' by Philip Buchan

'A Practical Guide to Health and Medical Cases in Immigration Law' by Rebecca Chapman & Miranda Butler

'A Practical Guide to Bad Character Evidence for Criminal Practitioners by Aparna Rao

'A Practical Guide to Extradition Law post-Brexit' by Myles Grandison et al

'A Practical Guide to Hoarding and Mental Health for Housing Lawyers' by Rachel Coyle

'Stephens on Contractual Indemnities' by Richard Stephens
'A Practical Guide to the EU Succession Regulation' by Richard Frimston
'A Practical Guide to Solicitor and Client Costs – Second Edition' by Robin Dunne
'Constructive Dismissal – Practice Pointers and Principles' by Benjimin Burgher
'A Practical Guide to Religion and Belief Discrimination Claims in the Workplace' by Kashif Ali
'A Practical Guide to the Law of Medical Treatment Decisions' by Ben Troke
'Fundamental Dishonesty and QOCS in Personal Injury Proceedings: Law and Practice' by Jake Rowley
'A Practical Guide to the Law in Relation to School Exclusions' by Charlotte Hadfield & Alice de Coverley
'A Practical Guide to Divorce for the Silver Separators' by Karin Walker
'The Right to be Forgotten – The Law and Practical Issues' by Melissa Stock
'A Practical Guide to Planning Law and Rights of Way in National Parks, the Broads and AONBs' by James Maurici QC, James Neill et al
'A Practical Guide to Election Law' by Tom Tabori
'A Practical Guide to the Law in Relation to Surrogacy' by Andrew Powell
'A Practical Guide to Claims Arising from Fatal Accidents – Second Edition' by James Patience
'A Practical Guide to Asbestos Claims' by Jonathan Owen & Gareth McAloon
'A Practical Guide to Stamp Duty Land Tax in England and Northern Ireland' by Suzanne O'Hara
'A Practical Guide to the Law of Farming Partnerships' by Philip Whitcomb
'A Practical Guide to the Law of Unlawful Eviction and Harassment – Second Edition' by Stephanie Lovegrove
'A Practical Guide to Costs in Personal Injury Claims – Second Edition' by Matthew Hoe
'A Practical Guide to the General Data Protection Regulation (GDPR) – Second Edition' by Keith Markham
'A Practical Guide to Working with Litigants in Person and McKenzie Friends in Family Cases' by Stuart Barlow
'Protecting Unregistered Brands: A Practical Guide to the Law of Passing Off' by Lorna Brazell
'A Practical Guide to Secondary Liability and Joint Enterprise Post-Jogee' by Joanne Cecil & James Mehigan

'A Practical Guide to the Pre-Action RTA Claims Protocol for Personal Injury Lawyers' by Antonia Ford

'A Practical Guide to Neighbour Disputes and the Law' by Alexander Walsh

'A Practical Guide to Coercive Control for Legal Practitioners and Victims' by Rachel Horman

'A Practical Guide to the Law of Driverless Cars – Second Edition'

by Alex Glassbrook, Emma Northey & Scarlett Milligan

'A Practical Guide to TOLATA Claims' by Greg Williams

'A Practical Guide to Elderly Law – Second Edition' by Justin Patten

'A Practical Guide to Responding to Housing Disrepair and Unfitness Claims' by Iain Wightwick

'A Practical Guide to the Law of Bullying and Harassment in the Workplace' by Philip Hyland

'How to Be a Freelance Solicitor: A Practical Guide to the SRA-Regulated Freelance Solicitor Model' by Paul Bennett

'A Practical Guide to Prison Injury Claims' by Malcolm Johnson

'A Practical Guide to Advising Clients at the Police Station' by Colin Stephen McKeown-Beaumont

'A Practical Guide to Antisocial Behaviour Injunctions – Second Edition' by Iain Wightwick

'Practical Mediation: A Guide for Mediators, Advocates, Advisers, Lawyers, and Students in Civil, Commercial, Business, Property, Workplace, and Employment Cases' by Jonathan Dingle with John Sephton

'The Mini-Pupillage Workbook' by David Boyle

'A Practical Guide to Crofting Law' by Brian Inkster

'A Practical Guide to the Law of Domain Names and Cybersquatting' by Andrew Clemson

'A Practical Guide to the Law of Gender Pay Gap Reporting' by Harini Iyengar

'NHS Whistleblowing and the Law' by Joseph England

'Employment Law and the Gig Economy' by Nigel Mackay & Annie Powell

'A Practical Guide to Noise Induced Hearing Loss (NIHL) Claims' by Andrew Mckie, Ian Skeate, Gareth McAloon

'An Introduction to Beauty Negligence Claims – A Practical Guide for the Personal Injury Practitioner' by Greg Almond

'Intercompany Agreements for Transfer Pricing Compliance' by Paul Sutton

'Zen and the Art of Mediation' by Martin Plowman

'A Practical Guide to Adoption for Family Lawyers' by Graham Pegg

'A Practical Guide to Industrial Disease Claims' by Andrew Mckie & Ian Skeate

'A Practical Guide to Conducting a Sheriff Court Proof' by Andrew Stevenson

'A Practical Guide to Vicarious Liability' by Mariel Irvine

'A Practical Guide to Applications for Landlord's Consent and Variation of Leases' by Mark Shelton

'A Practical Guide to Relief from Sanctions Post-Mitchell and Denton' by Peter Causton

'A Practical Guide to Equity Release for Advisors' by Paul Sams

'A Practical Guide to Financial Services Claims' by Chris Hegarty

'A Practical Guide to Financial Ombudsman Service Claims' by Adam Temple & Robert Scrivenor

'A Practical Guide to Running Housing Disrepair and Cavity Wall Claims – Second Edition' by Andrew Mckie & Ian Skeate

'A Practical Guide to Holiday Sickness Claims – Second Edition' by Andrew Mckie & Ian Skeate

'Arguments and Tactics for Personal Injury and Clinical Negligence Claims' by Dorian Williams

'A Practical Guide to Drone Law' by Rufus Ballaster, Andrew Firman, Eleanor Clot

'On Experts: CPR35 for Lawyers and Experts' by David Boyle

'An Introduction to Personal Injury Law' by David Boyle

These books and more are available to order online direct from the publisher at www.lawbriefpublishing.com, where you can also read free sample chapters. For any queries, call us on 0844 587 2383 or email us at mail@lawbriefpublishing.com.

Our books are all generally in stock at www.amazon.co.uk with free next day delivery for Prime members, and at good legal bookshops such as Wildy & Sons.

We are regularly launching new books in our series of practical day-to-day practitioners' guides. Visit our website and join our free newsletter to be kept informed and to receive special offers, free chapters, etc.

You can also follow us on Twitter at www.twitter.com/lawbriefpub.

www.ingramcontent.com/pod-product-compliance
Lightning Source LLC
LaVergne TN
LVHW022044200926
848481LV00003B/788
* 9 7 8 1 9 1 6 6 9 8 6 1 1 *